## Other books by Akili Kumasi

*Fatherhood Principles of Joseph the Carpenter:*
*Examples of Godly Fatherhood*

*On the Outside Looking In:*
*Hope for Separated Fathers Who Want to Be Good Fathers*

*Fun Meals for Fathers and Sons:*
*Recipes and Activities for Bonding & Mentoring*

*Bible Word Search Puzzles Book Series*
*Vol. I: Extracts from the Bible*
*Vol. II: Women in the Bible*
*Vol. III: Fathers in the Bible*
*Vol. IV: Prayers in the Bible*
*Vol. V: Victories in the Bible*
*Vol. VI: Parables in the Bible*
*Vol. VII: Promises in the Bible*

*Christian Word Search Puzzles:*
*Vol. One: Foundations in the Bible*

*101 In the Bible – Scriptures and Lessons Series:*
*101 Women in the Bible*
*101 Prayers in the Bible*
*101 Victories in the Bible*

# God's Healing Scriptures:

## 240 Prayers and Promises for Healing in the Bible

Complied by

# Akili Kumasi

## G.I.L. PUBLICATIONS
New York, New York

www.GILpublications.com

# God's Healing Scriptures:
## 240 Prayers and Promises For Healing in the Bible

Copyright 2014 by G.I.L. Publications
A division of The God Is Love Ministries

ISBN-13: 978-1494845476
ISBN-10: 1494845474

Library of Congress Catalog Number: 2013958431

Scriptures marked "KJV" are taken from the King James Version of the Bible.

Scriptures marked "NIV" are taken from the New International Version of the Bible Scripture taken from the Holy Bible, NEW INTERNATIONAL VERSION®. Copyright © 1973, 1978, 1984 International Bible Society. All rights reserved throughout the world. Used by permission of International Bible Society. NEW INTERNATIONAL VERSION® and NIV® are registered trademarks of International Bible Society. Use of either trademark for the offering of goods or services requires the prior written consent of International Bible Society.

Scripture quotations marked "NLT" are taken from the Holy Bible, New Living Translation, copyright © 1996. Used by permission of Tyndale House Publishers, Inc., Wheaton, Illinois 60189. All rights reserved.

Scripture marked "AMP" (AMP®) are taken from the Amplified® Bible. Scripture quotations taken from the Amplified® Bible, Copyright © 1954, 1958, 1962, 1964, 1965, 1987 by The Lockman Foundation. Used by permission." (www.Lockman.org)

Scriptures marked as "CEV" are taken from the Contemporary English Version Copyright © 1995 by American Bible Society. Used by permission.

All scripture quotes are in bold and italicized.

Update #2: 140703

Cover Photograph © Dmytro Tolokonov (#20003663), www.fotolia.com.

## G.I.L. PUBLICATIONS
### THE GOD IS LOVE MINISTRIES
P. O. Box 80275, Brooklyn, NY 11208
info@GILpublications.com
www.GILpublications.com
www.GodsHealingScripturesBook.com

# Table of Contents

Introduction ........................................................... 11
Why Should We Study God's Word on Healing? ..... 17
Healing Promises From The Old Testament .......... 27
Healing Promises From The New Testament .......... 45
Healing Examples From The Old Testament .......... 49

   1. Abraham's Body Restored ...................................... 49
   2. Sarah's Womb Restored, Isaac Was Born ............. 49
   3. Abimelech, His Wife and Maidservants Healed (Abraham) ............................................................ 51
   4. Isaac Prayed, Rebekah's Womb Restored, Jacob and Esau Born ........................................... 53
   5. Rachel's Womb Restored, Joseph Born ................. 54
   6. Moses Leprous Hand Restored ............................. 54
   7. Mariam Healed From Leprosy .............................. 55
   8. Aaron Stopped Plague Which Had Killed 14,700 .................................................................. 56
   9. Serpent of Brass Used to Heal From Snake Bites ..................................................................... 57
 10. The Lord Sustained Joshua in the Dessert ............ 58
 11. Manoah's Wife's Womb Restored, Samson Born ...................................................................... 58
 12. Hannah's Womb Restored, Samuel Born ............... 60
 13. Return of Ark Brings Healing for Philistines .......... 63
 14. David Sinned – Plagued Stopped After 70,000 Die ........................................................................ 63
 15. King Jeroboam's Withered Hand Restored ............ 65
 16. Son of the Widow of Zarephath Brought Back to Life (Elijah) ....................................................... 66
 17. King Ahaziah Did Not Get Healed ........................ 66
 18. Water Healed (Elisha) ........................................... 67

## Table of Contents

19. Shunammite Woman's Womb Restored, Son Born (Elisha) ...................................................... 68
20. Shunammite Woman's Son Raised From The Dead (Elisha) .................................................... 69
21. Healing for Death in the Pot (Elisha) ...................... 70
22. Naaman Cleansed of Leprosy (Elisha) ................... 71
23. Dead Man Revived in Elisha's Tomb ..................... 73
24. Terminally Ill King Hezekiah Had 15 Years Added to His Life (Isaiah) ....................................... 73
25. King Asa Ignored God – Did Not Get Healed ........... 76
26. King Uzziah's Sin Caused Leprosy ........................ 77
27. King Hezekiah Prayed for Israel's Healing .............. 78
28. Job Repented and Prayed for His Friends, He Was Restored .................................................... 78
29. David Healed ..................................................... 80
30. Nebuchadnezzar Punished With Insanity, Then Healed ............................................................. 80
31. Israel Healed ..................................................... 81

## Healing Examples From The New Testament: The Gospels ............................................. 82

1. Jesus Teaches, Preaches and Heals In Synagogues in Galilee ......................................... 82
2. Jesus Cures Man With Leprosy ............................ 84
3. Jesus Heals the Roman Centurion's Servant ......... 86
4. Jesus Heals Peter's Mother-In-Law ....................... 87
5. Jesus Heals Many Sick in the Evening at Peter's House in Capernaum ............................... 88
6. Jesus Casts Demons Into Herd of Pigs .................. 89
7. Jesus Forgives and Heals Paralytic Lowered Through the Roof .............................................. 92
8. Jesus Raises Jarius' Daughter (Synagogue Leader) ............................................................ 95
9. Jesus Cures Woman With the Issue of Blood ......... 97
10. Jesus Gives Sight to Two Blind Men .................... 99
11. Jesus Heals Mute Demonic ................................ 100

## Table of Contents

12. Jesus Teaching, Preaching and Healing Every Sickness and Disease ......... 100
13. Jesus Sends the Twelve Disciples to Preach and Heal ......... 100
14. Jesus Healed Many – Answers John the Baptist's Disciples ......... 102
15. Jesus Heals Man with a Withered Hand ......... 103
16. Jesus Heals Many By the Sea ......... 105
17. Jesus Heals the Blind and Mute Demoniac ......... 106
18. Jesus Did Few Miracles Because of Their Lack of Faith ......... 108
19. Jesus Heals Their Sick (Before Feeding the 5,000) ......... 108
20. Jesus Heals Many at Gennesaret ......... 109
21. Jesus Heals the Canaanite Woman's Demon-Possessed Daughter ......... 110
22. Lame, Blind, Maimed, Mute Laid at Jesus Feet ... 111
23. Jesus Heals the Boy With a Demon (Seizures) ..... 111
24. Jesus Restores of Sight to Blind Bartimaeus on the Side of the Road ......... 114
25. People Rose From Dead When Jesus Gave Up His Spirit – and After Jesus' Resurrection ......... 115
26. Jesus Drives Out Evil Spirit from Mad Man in Synagogue in Capernaum ......... 116
27. Jesus Appointed Twelve ......... 117
28. Jesus Heals Deaf and Dumb Man ......... 118
29. Jesus Restores Sight to Blind Man at Bethsaida ......... 118
30. Man Was Raised From The Dead ......... 119
31. Seven Demons Driven from Mary Magdalene (and Other Women) ......... 119
32. Disciples Preach and Work Signs After Jesus' Ascension ......... 120
33. Elizabeth's Womb Restored, John the Baptist Born ......... 120
34. Jesus Raises Widow's Dead Son at Nain ......... 122
35. Jesus Sent Out the Seventy-Two ......... 123

Table of Contents

36. Jesus Heals Woman Crippled For 18 Years (on the Sabbath) ...................................................... 124
37. Jesus Heals Man With Dropsy (on the Sabbath) .............................................................. 124
38. Jesus Cleanses Ten Leprous Men ...................... 125
39. Jesus Restores Malchus' Ear at Gethsemane ....... 126
40. Jesus Heals Royal Official's Son ......................... 127
41. Jesus Heals the Invalid at Pool of Bethsaida ........ 128
42. Jesus Heals Man Born Blind .............................. 129
43. Jesus Raises Lazarus From the Dead ................. 130
44. Jesus Is Resurrected from the Dead ................... 133

## Healing Examples From The New Testament: The Book of Acts and The Epistles ............. 142

1. Man at the Gate of Beautiful Healed (Peter with John) ....................................................... 142
2. Apostles Stretched For Their Hands To Heal ........ 143
3. Apostles Do Signs and Wonders, People Healed Who Fell Under Peter's Shadow .......................... 143
4. Great Wonders and Miracles Through Stephen .... 144
5. Phillip's Mission Included Healing ...................... 144
6. Ananias Laid Hands on Saul (Paul), His Sight Restored ......................................................... 144
7. Aeneas Healed of Palsy (Paralysis) (Peter) ............ 145
8. Tabitha (Dorcas) Raised From Death To Life (Peter) ............................................................ 145
9. Jesus Healed All That Were Possessed of The Devil .............................................................. 146
10. In Iconium, God Confirmed His Word Through Signs & Wonders by Paul and Barnabas ............. 147
11. Healing for a Man Lame From Birth at Lystra (Paul) ............................................................. 147
12. Evil Spirit Driven From Damsel (Paul) ................. 148
13. People Healed By Paul Sending His Handkerchiefs or Aprons ..................................... 148
14. Sons of Sceva Failed to Drive Out Evil Spirit ....... 148
15. Eutychus Raised Back to Life (Paul) .................... 149

## Table of Contents

16. Was Paul Healed – Or Raised from the Dead? ..... 150
17. Paul Exhibits Immunity to Viper's Bite ................ 150
18. Publius' Father Healed of Fever and Bloody Diarrhea (Paul) .................................................. 151
19. Others Healed of Diseases On Island of Malta (Paul) ................................................................ 151
20. Abraham and Sarah's Bodies Restored Through Faith .................................................. 151
21. Sarah Given Strength to Conceive, Abraham's Body Restored .................................................. 152

## Examples of Barren Women & Miraculous Births .................................................................. 154

1. Sarah's Womb Restored, Isaac Was Born ........... 154
2. Abraham and Sarah's Bodies Restored Through Faith .................................................. 155
3. Sarah Given Strength to Conceive, Abraham's Body Restored .................................................. 156
4. Abimelech, His Wife and Maidservants Healed (Abraham) ......................................................... 157
5. Isaac Prayed, Rebekah's Womb Restored, Jacob and Esau Born ........................................ 158
6. Rachel's Womb Restored, Joseph Born ............. 159
7. Manoah's Wife's Womb Restored, Samson Born .................................................................. 160
8. Hannah's Womb Restored, Samuel Born ........... 162
9. Shunammite Woman's Womb Restored, Son Born (Elisha) ..................................................... 164
10. Elizabeth's Womb Restored, John the Baptist Born .................................................................. 165
11. Mary, the Mother of Jesus ................................ 168

## People Raised From the Dead ........................... 170

1. Son of the Widow of Zarephath Brought Back to Life (Elijah) .................................................. 170
2. Shunammite Woman's Son Raised From The Dead (Elisha) .................................................. 171

## Table of Contents

3. Dead Man Revived in Elisha's Tomb ..................... 173
4. Jesus Raises Jarius' Daughter (Synagogue Leader) ........................................................... 173
5. People Rose From Dead When Jesus Gave Up His Spirit – and After Jesus' Resurrection ........... 176
6. Jesus Is Resurrected from the Dead .................... 176
7. Man Was Raised From The Dead ........................ 176
8. Jesus Raises Widow's Dead Son at Nain .............. 177
9. Jesus Raises Lazarus From the Dead .................. 177
10. Tabitha (Dorcas) Raised From Death To Life (Peter) ............................................................... 180
11. Eutychus Raised Back to Life (Paul) .................... 181
12. Was Paul Healed – Or Raised from the Dead? ...... 182

*Introduction*

Herein is a book of God's Healing Scriptures.

When I sat down to write an introduction to the scriptures in this book, I found it to be more challenging than I thought it would be. There is a lot to say on this topic and quite frankly, the subject is too large and too controversial to sum it all up in a few pages. The best thing that I can do is start with why I compiled these scriptures into a book in the first place.

**What is the Purpose of This Book?**

Quite often I found myself searching the Bible, other Biblical books and the Bible websites for healing scriptures. However, I was never able to find all of the scriptures on healing in one place. This made studying the scriptures very difficult. I kept taking notes, making lists, printing pages, making copies and marking favorites. Eventually I accumulated a massive amount of unorganized paper thrown into multiple file folders. I three-hole punched all of this and organized it into a binder. It became apparent that my efforts were often over-lapping and many times I had even duplicated exactly what I had done on a previously occasion when searching God's Word on healing.

Since I was doing all of this - I was sure that others were doing it as well - because God's Word on healing is so enormous and there is a great thirst to know and understand what God has said to His people. I began to envision a book that would contain all of the scriptures on Divine healing for everyone's easy access. Thus, a book concept was born, one that would be available in print and electronically online as an e-book in various forms. Since

Introduction

God had led me to study the scriptures, I believe He also led me to compile this book.

So the first purpose of this book is to be a research tool for those who want to find and read God's Healing Scriptures.

The second purpose for this book is to aid us in our quest to know the truth about God's Healing Promise. There are many theories, but there is only one truth. If we are to truly follow what God has in mind for us on healing then we must know the truth and this can only be accomplished through the study of His Word.

Jesus told us that God's **Word is truth** (John 17:17). He also told us that:

> *"If ye continue in my word, then are ye my disciples indeed; And ye shall know the truth, and the truth shall make you free.*
> John 8:26-32 KJV

The third purpose for this book is to be a tool to help us build our faith – remember - **faith cometh by hearing, and hearing by the word of God** (Romans 10:17 KJV).

Read it, study it, meditate on it – and pray.

## How to Use This Book

First, in many instances the verses of scripture contained herein need to be examined in the context of the particular message of the chapter in the Bible where the scriptures come from. By examining the scriptures in this manner, we can understand the message of the Bible verses in their historical and spiritual context – and thus we are able to apply God's Word in a modern context more appropriately.

Second, it is suggested that you check scriptures of particular interest in at least three different translations of the Bible to see how different versions present specific concepts. It is also important to check the original Hebrew and Greek text to see the original words used and their meanings.

Third, it is a good idea to read the scriptures out loud as this increases your attention span and it can help you take in God's Word through your hearing – which is (as stated above) a method to increase faith.

Fourth, stand up in a well-lit room. There is something about reading God's word in this fashion that gives us a purposefulness. It also helps us to maintain an alertness to what we are doing and what God is saying.

Fifth, take the scriptures as medicine. If you or someone else is sick, grab hold of the scriptures that resonate with you from herein and place your hand on that spot on the body and pray God's promises (in faith) from those scriptures - three times a day. God's Word is medicine (Proverbs 4:22). We should use it as such.

## What Scriptures are Included in This Book?

This book is divided into several sections. First, an article, *"Why Should We Study God's Word on Healing?"* Second, the promises of God's healing from both the Old Testament and the New Testament. In this book we talk about healing "promises." However, there is really only one "promise" and that is that God is the God Who heals – He is **Yhôvâh Râphā** (Exodus 15:26). Third, the examples of healing from both the Old Testament and the New Testament. Lastly, we have included a repeat of the scriptures on Barren Women giving birth and those in Biblical history that were raised from the dead.

## Introduction

For the most part we have sought to include only scriptures that directly pertain to Divine healing. That is, the healings that were the result of God's Divine will and intervention.

Many scriptures (but not all) that just pertain to God's delegated authority to us or His promise to answer our prayers and His other awesome promises were intentionally not included – because in some instances those scriptures (although very powerful) are far too general (i.e. I John 5:14-15) and do not specifically address the question of Divine healing – which is the topic we want to keep the focus on.

In some instances, included herein are scriptures related to practices for good health. Medical healing is only briefly mentioned (i.e. Jeremiah 8:22 where God used a metaphor of medical healing to discuss spiritual healing).

There are scriptures included herein where healing did not take place – because there is something to learn even when God does not heal (i.e. King Ahaziah in II Kings 1:1-4, 15-17 or the devastation of the Sons of Sceva in Acts 19:13-19).

The scriptures contained herein are taken from the King James Version of the Bible (KJV) for the simple reason that the KJV is in public domain and can be quoted from extensively without copyright infringement. As stated above the scriptures should be checked in multiple versions and in the Hebrew and Greek original texts.

The scriptures (in each section) are listed in the order in which they appear in the Bible, with the exception of the section on Barren Women.

## **Further Study**

We mentioned above that Divine healing is an enormous topic. It is one that cannot be summed up all in one volume.

## Introduction

With this book, we simply sought to present God's Word on Divine healing and let the Holy Spirit do the talking to those who will study, meditate and pray on God's Word.

*A serious student of Divine healing will delineate the scriptures herein into types, methods and purposes for further study and meditation.*

Another area of study would be to examine all the theories, practices or claims of healing from the past or present in light of the scriptures. Much work has been done by noted authors in this area already.

I pray that the scriptures in this book will be illuminating for everyone who will avail themselves of them.

God Bless You All, In Jesus' Precious Name!

Akili Kumasi
God Is Love Ministries
New York, New York

January 2014

# Why Should We Study God's Word on Healing?

Below are seven reasons why we should study God's Word on healing.

### (1)  God Heals.

Of that, there is no question.  God Heals!  He told us so in His Word.

> *. . . I am the Lord that healeth thee.*
>                                             Exodus 15:26

The original Hebrew text for God's Name in Exodus 15:26 is **Yhôvâh Râphā** (Jehovah Rapha).  When translated into English these Hebrews words, Jehovah Rapha, mean, "*I am the Lord Who Heals.*"

> **Yhôvâh**   (H#3068) means *self existent or eternal, the proper name of the one true God, Jehovah, the Lord.*
>
> **Râphā**    (H#7495) means *to mend, to cure, cause to heal, physician, repair thoroughly, make whole.*[1]

When we study the Names of God we find that His Names describe His character, Who He is and what He does.  Since God is unchanging - He is the same, yesterday, today and tomorrow (Malachi 3:6; James 1:17).  Therefore, Who He was

---

[1] James Strong, *Strong's Exhaustive Concordance of the Bible.*

yesterday – *IS* - Who He is today.  He healed yesterday, thus He heals today!  This is an unavoidable Biblical fact.  How He heals might change, when He heals might change – but, the fact that He heals does not change because that is Who He is.

There is a wide range of healings recorded in the Bible.  However, generally, when we think of Divine healing we might first envision the miraculous physical healings performed by Jesus and recorded in the four Gospels.  But, these were not the only types of healings, nor were they the first healings.

The Old Testament had its share of healings as well, with at least Abraham, Isaac, Elijah, Elisha and Isaiah having prayed for those who received healing.  In the New Testament, Jesus, Peter, Paul, and the rest of the disciples (including Judas Iscariot), plus Stephen, Philip and Barnabas were used by God to administer healing.

Some of those healings were not just physical. Some people were demon-possessed which led to physical or mental sickness. For example, the man in the tombs with the legion of demons that Jesus cast into the herd of pigs in Luke 8:26-39.  He was mentally ill with no apparent physical impairment.  The possessed-boy whose father took him to Jesus in Mark 9:14-29 suffered from seizures.  He had both demon-possession and physical affliction.

Clearly, there were different types of healings. Since humans have a spirit, a soul and a body (I Thessalonians 5:23) – healings took place on all three levels.  There were also instances of multiple healings at once (the multitude reached out to Jesus in Matthew 8:16-17, many touched the hem of his garment and were healed in Matthew 14:34-36 and Peter's shadow fell on many in Acts 5:15). There was healing for the people in general (II Chronicles 30:15-20). The Bible even talked about healing for the land (II Chronicles 7:14) and for the water (II Kings 2:14-22) that was used for God's people.

## (2) God Showed His Healing Power and Promise Throughout the Bible

Throughout Biblical history (at least since Abraham), God demonstrated His ability to heal, His willingness to heal and His commitment to heal the sick. He used at least three different methods to heal (both in the Old and New Testaments): (1) He healed directly through His own miraculously intervention, (2) He healed through human agents, and (3) He healed through medical or natural means.

## (3) However, Questions Still Remain

Even though we see clearly in God's Word, from both His promise and His practice, that He heals, questions about Divine healing still remain in the Church today.

- Is Divine healing a conditional promise?
- Is Divine healing only for God's people?
- Is Divine healing only for people without sin?
- How does God heal?
- When God heal?
- Through whom does God heal?
- Under what circumstances does God heal?
- Did God heal just to relieve a sick person of bad health?
- What was God's purpose for healing?
- Should we believe that God's purpose today for healing is any different from what it was in the past?
- What type of healings does God do today?

These questions and many others persist because for the most part - we do not understand God's healing promise. That is, we do not understand His promise in Biblical terms

– and – we do not understand when His promise applies to our situation, or when it does not and why.  We might have faith in God's ability to heal, but to understand why and when He heals is a mystery.  As such, many devote Christians even doubt and/or deny God's healing power and His promise.

That is why this book is important.

## (4)  God Is Sovereign!

God in his sovereignty decides when to heal and who to heal. He has His purpose and His reasons.  He does not need to answer to anyone.

We as God's people must come to Him to petition for our needs.  Even though we can come in confidence (Hebrews 4:16), God is still sovereign.  He makes the decision to heal or not to heal.

By studying, meditating and praying on God healing scriptures we can better understand and be better led by the Holy Spirit to pray in God's will.  Thus when we pray we are better lined up with God's purpose and His will – and our prayers will more readily be answered[2] – and we can best be used by God for His purpose.

## (5)  We Must Seek the Truth From God's Word

Since questions (and doubt) remain about God's healing promise, we must study His Word so that the truth can be revealed to us by the Holy Spirit.

---

[2] Keep in mind that not only do our prayers need to be lined-up with God's will – but our hearts must also be right (James 4:3).  R. A. Torrey has an excellent little (put powerful) book on prayer called, *How to Pray*. In the chapter, "Hindrances to Prayer" he explains seven roadblocks from scripture that can prevent our prayers from being answered!

## Why Should We Study God's Word on Healing?

When we do not know the truth of God's Word we are susceptible to error – either in one direction (or extreme) or in the other direction. That is, we could put too much emphasis on healing and alleged power - or - we could not put enough emphasis and confidence in God's healing promise and thus reject God's power to heal.

Let us examine an important scripture where God's people were in error because of their lack of knowledge of God.

In Hosea we are told by God that:

> ***My people are destroyed for lack of knowledge . . .***
>
> Hoses 4:6a

Our first lesson from Hosea 4:6 is that a lack of knowledge (of God and His Word) can lead us to be destroyed. Thus, we have the responsibility to know God and His Word – so that we can function properly as believers, as His people.

Look further at this verse:

> ***My people are destroyed for lack of knowledge:***
> ***because thou hast rejected knowledge . . .***
>
> Hosea 4:6a-b

Here we see the second lesson from this verse above, that God's people not only lacked knowledge, but they had rejected obtaining knowledge as well. This was a twofold problem, one with the people and the other with the priests.

So the responsibility here is for both the people and the priests (today – the pastors, priests, preachers and teachers etc.) to seek God's truth, to not be satisfied with a lack of knowledge. We should not even be satisfied with a little bit of knowledge. We must seek *ALL* of God's truth!

Let us look even further at this verse:

> **My people are destroyed for lack of knowledge:**
> **because thou hast rejected knowledge,**
> **I will also reject thee,**
> **that thou shalt be no priest to me:**
> **seeing thou hast forgotten the law of thy God,**
> **I will also forget thy children.**
>
> Hosea 4:6

The third lesson from this scripture is that God has a consequence for us rejecting His knowledge, because to reject His knowledge is to reject Him.

Our responsibility then is threefold: (1) our pastors, priests, preachers, and teachers must teach God's Word to God's people; (2) they must seek the truth, not just some warmed over theories which have not been researched and studied by God's people, and (3) according to Acts 17:11 God's people must know (or check) the scriptures to verify that what our leaders say is accurate. We must study and know God's Word for ourselves!

> **Now the Berean Jews were of more noble character than those in Thessalonica, for they received the message with great eagerness and examined the Scriptures every day to see if what Paul said was true.**
>
> Acts 17:11 NIV

Thus, we must study God's Word on healing so that we can do things properly and in order.

## (6) Having Sought and Received the Truth of God's Word, We Must Stand On It

When a believer truly seeks God's truth, he or she will definitely find it:

> *But if from thence thou shalt seek the Lord thy God, thou shalt find him, if thou seek him with all thy heart and with all thy soul.*
> Deuteronomy 4:29

Under these circumstances (diligently seeking God's truth) our faith will (by definition) be increased. God tells us so:

> *So then faith cometh by hearing, and hearing by the word of God.*
> Romans 10:17

Now armed with the truth of God's Word and faith in God's Word – we must stand – or act on God's Word. In James, we are taught that:

> *14 What doth it profit, my brethren, though a man say he hath faith, and have not works? can faith save him?*
>
> *17 Even so faith, if it hath not works, is dead, being alone.*
>
> *19 Thou believest that there is one God; thou doest well: the devils also believe, and tremble.*
> *20 But wilt thou know, O vain man, that faith without works is dead?*
> *21 Was not Abraham our father justified by works, when he had offered Isaac his son upon the altar?*

***²² Seest thou how faith wrought with his works, and by works was faith made perfect?***
***²³ And the scripture was fulfilled which saith, Abraham believed God, and it was imputed unto him for righteousness: and he was called the Friend of God.***
***²⁴ Ye see then how that by works a man is justified, and not by faith only.***
James 2:14, 17, 19-24

Verse 22 above is of particular potency - **by works was faith made perfect**. Let us examine this phrase more deeply by comparing the KJV to other versions:

The New International Version of the Bible (NIV) reads:

> **. . . and his faith was made complete by what he did.**
James 2:22 (NIV)

The New Living Translation of the Bible (NLT) reads:

> **His actions made his faith complete.**
James 2:22 (NLT)

The Amplified Bible (AMP) reads:

> **. . . and [his] faith was completed and reached its supreme expression [when he implemented it] by [good] works.**
James 2:22 (AMP)

The Contemporary English Version of the Bible (CEV) reads:

> ***He proved that his faith was real by what he did.***
>
> James 2:22 (CEV)

WOW! What a scripture! What a truth to internalize!

Since there is a call to action here, it is very important that we understand God's Word correctly, so that we do not go off half-cocked or poorly informed. Look at the differences in how that one phrase is portrayed by different teams of translators. I especially like the last one, the CEV, ***He proved that his faith was real by what he did***. In other words, Abraham's faith was not real unless he acted on what he believed. If He did nothing then his faith was not real!

Is your faith real? Seriously, are you willing to really go deep into God's Word and stand on it?

## (7) What Next?

Get started! Dig in! This book of scriptures is for your study, meditation and prayer. Read it, mark it up, re-read it, verify it, let it point you in the direction of deeper and more thorough research into God's Word, refer back to portions of it when needed. In short, use it as the Holy Spirit directs you to do so.

I pray that you will be led by God as you examine the scriptures with eagerness!

God Bless You All, In Jesus' Precious Name!

Akili Kumasi
God Is Love Ministries
New York, New York

January 2014

# *Healing Promises From The Old Testament*

## Exodus 15:26

26 And said, If thou wilt diligently hearken to the voice of the Lord thy God, and wilt do that which is right in his sight, and wilt give ear to his commandments, and keep all his statutes, I will put none of these diseases upon thee, which I have brought upon the Egyptians: for I am the Lord that healeth thee.

## Exodus 23:23-26

23 For mine Angel shall go before thee, and bring thee in unto the Amorites, and the Hittites, and the Perizzites, and the Canaanites, the Hivites, and the Jebusites: and I will cut them off.
24 Thou shalt not bow down to their gods, nor serve them, nor do after their works: but thou shalt utterly overthrow them, and quite break down their images.
25 And ye shall serve the Lord your God, and he shall bless thy bread, and thy water; and I will take sickness away from the midst of thee.
26 There shall nothing cast their young, nor be barren, in thy land: the number of thy days I will fulfil.

## Deuteronomy 7:14-15

14 Thou shalt be blessed above all people: there shall not be male or female barren among you, or among your cattle.
15 And the Lord will take away from thee all sickness, and will put none of the evil diseases of Egypt, which thou

knowest, upon thee; but will lay them upon all them that hate thee.

## Deuteronomy 11:9, 21

9 And that ye may prolong your days in the land, which the Lord sware unto your fathers to give unto them and to their seed, a land that floweth with milk and honey.

21 That your days may be multiplied, and the days of your children, in the land which the Lord sware unto your fathers to give them, as the days of heaven upon the earth.

## Deuteronomy 28:1-4, 11, 15, 27, 35, 58-61

1 And it shall come to pass, if thou shalt hearken diligently unto the voice of the Lord thy God, to observe and to do all his commandments which I command thee this day, that the Lord thy God will set thee on high above all nations of the earth:
2 And all these blessings shall come on thee, and overtake thee, if thou shalt hearken unto the voice of the Lord thy God.
3 Blessed shalt thou be in the city, and blessed shalt thou be in the field.
4 Blessed shall be the fruit of thy body, and the fruit of thy ground, and the fruit of thy cattle, the increase of thy kine, and the flocks of thy sheep.

11 And the Lord shall make thee plenteous in goods, in the fruit of thy body, and in the fruit of thy cattle, and in the fruit of thy ground, in the land which the Lord sware unto thy fathers to give thee.

15 But it shall come to pass, if thou wilt not hearken unto the voice of the Lord thy God, to observe to do all his commandments and his statutes which I command thee this

day; that all these curses shall come upon thee, and overtake thee:

27 The Lord will smite thee with the botch of Egypt, and with the emerods, and with the scab, and with the itch, whereof thou canst not be healed.

35 The Lord shall smite thee in the knees, and in the legs, with a sore botch that cannot be healed, from the sole of thy foot unto the top of thy head.

58 If you do not carefully follow all the words of this law, which are written in this book, and do not revere this glorious and awesome name—the Lord your God— 59 the Lord will send fearful plagues on you and your descendants, harsh and prolonged disasters, and severe and lingering illnesses. 60 He will bring on you all the diseases of Egypt that you dreaded, and they will cling to you. 61 The Lord will also bring on you every kind of sickness and disaster not recorded in this Book of the Law, until you are destroyed.

## Deuteronomy 30:19-20

19 I call heaven and earth to record this day against you, that I have set before you life and death, blessing and cursing: therefore choose life, that both thou and thy seed may live:
20 That thou mayest love the Lord thy God, and that thou mayest obey his voice, and that thou mayest cleave unto him: for he is thy life, and the length of thy days: that thou mayest dwell in the land which the Lord sware unto thy fathers, to Abraham, to Isaac, and to Jacob, to give them.

## Deuteronomy 32:39

39 See now that I, even I, am he, and there is no god with me: I kill, and I make alive; I wound, and I heal: neither is there any that can deliver out of my hand.

## II Chronicles 6:26-31

26 When the heaven is shut up, and there is no rain, because they have sinned against thee; yet if they pray toward this place, and confess thy name, and turn from their sin, when thou dost afflict them;
27 Then hear thou from heaven, and forgive the sin of thy servants, and of thy people Israel, when thou hast taught them the good way, wherein they should walk; and send rain upon thy land, which thou hast given unto thy people for an inheritance.
28 If there be dearth in the land, if there be pestilence, if there be blasting, or mildew, locusts, or caterpillers; if their enemies besiege them in the cities of their land; whatsoever sore or whatsoever sickness there be:
29 Then what prayer or what supplication soever shall be made of any man, or of all thy people Israel, when every one shall know his own sore and his own grief, and shall spread forth his hands in this house:
30 Then hear thou from heaven thy dwelling place, and forgive, and render unto every man according unto all his ways, whose heart thou knowest; (for thou only knowest the hearts of the children of men:)
31 That they may fear thee, to walk in thy ways, so long as they live in the land which thou gavest unto our fathers.

## II Chronicles 7:14

14 If my people, which are called by my name, shall humble themselves, and pray, and seek my face, and turn from their wicked ways; then will I hear from heaven, and will forgive their sin, and will heal their land.

## II Chronicles 20:9

9 If, when evil cometh upon us, as the sword, judgment, or pestilence, or famine, we stand before this house, and in thy presence, (for thy name is in this house,) and cry unto thee in our affliction, then thou wilt hear and help.

Healing Promises From The Old Testament

## Nehemiah 8:10

[10] Then he said unto them, Go your way, eat the fat, and drink the sweet, and send portions unto them for whom nothing is prepared: for this day is holy unto our Lord: neither be ye sorry; for the joy of the Lord is your strength.

## Job 5:18

[18] For he maketh sore, and bindeth up: he woundeth, and his hands make whole.

## Psalm 6:2

[2] Have mercy upon me, O Lord; for I am weak: O Lord, heal me; for my bones are vexed.

## Psalm 29:11

[11] The Lord will give strength unto his people; the Lord will bless his people with peace.

## Psalm 30:2

[2] O Lord my God, I cried unto thee, and thou hast healed me.

## Psalm 34:19-20

[19] Many are the afflictions of the righteous: but the Lord delivereth him out of them all.
[20] He keepeth all his bones: not one of them is broken.

## Psalm 41:1-4

[1] Blessed is he that considereth the poor: the Lord will deliver him in time of trouble.
[2] The Lord will preserve him, and keep him alive; and he shall be blessed upon the earth: and thou wilt not deliver him unto the will of his enemies.

3 The Lord will strengthen him upon the bed of languishing: thou wilt make all his bed in his sickness.
4 I said, Lord, be merciful unto me: heal my soul; for I have sinned against thee.

## Psalm 42:11 (v.5 & 43:5)

11 Why art thou cast down, O my soul? and why art thou disquieted within me? hope thou in God: for I shall yet praise him, who is the health of my countenance, and my God.

## Psalm 91:3

3 Surely he shall deliver thee from the snare of the fowler, and from the noisome (deadly-NIV) pestilence.

## Psalm 91:9-10

9 Because thou hast made the Lord, which is my refuge, even the most High, thy habitation;
10 There shall no evil befall thee, neither shall any plague come nigh thy dwelling.

## Psalm 103:1-5

1 Bless the Lord, O my soul: and all that is within me, bless his holy name.
2 Bless the Lord, O my soul, and forget not all his benefits:
3 Who forgiveth all thine iniquities; who healeth all thy diseases;
4 Who redeemeth thy life from destruction; who crowneth thee with lovingkindness and tender mercies;
5 Who satisfieth thy mouth with good things; so that thy youth is renewed like the eagle's.

## Psalm 107:19-20

19 Then they cry unto the Lord in their trouble, and he saveth them out of their distresses.

[20] He sent his word, and healed them, and delivered them from their destructions.

## Psalm 113:9

[9] He maketh the barren woman to keep house, and to be a joyful mother of children. Praise ye the Lord.

## Psalm 118:17-18

[7] I shall not die, but live, and declare the works of the Lord. [18] The Lord hath chastened me sore: but he hath not given me over unto death.

## Psalm 119:17

[17] Deal bountifully with thy servant, that I may live, and keep thy word.

## Psalm 119:116

[116] Uphold me according unto thy word, that I may live: and let me not be ashamed of my hope.

## Psalm 147:1-3

[1] Praise ye the Lord: for it is good to sing praises unto our God; for it is pleasant; and praise is comely.
[2] The Lord doth build up Jerusalem: he gathereth together the outcasts of Israel.
[3] He healeth the broken in heart, and bindeth up their wounds.

## Proverbs 3:1-2

[1] My son, forget not my law; but let thine heart keep my commandments:
[2] For length of days, and long life, and peace, shall they add to thee.

## Proverbs 3:7-8

7 Be not wise in thine own eyes: fear the Lord, and depart from evil.
8 It shall be health to thy navel, and marrow to thy bones.

## Proverbs 3:21-22

21 My son, let not them depart from thine eyes: keep sound wisdom and discretion:
22 So shall they be life unto thy soul, and grace to thy neck.

## Proverbs 4:10

10 Hear, O my son, and receive my sayings; and the years of thy life shall be many.

## Proverbs 4:20-23

20 My son, attend to my words; incline thine ear unto my sayings.
21 Let them not depart from thine eyes; keep them in the midst of thine heart.
22 For they are life unto those that find them, and health to all their flesh.
23 Keep thy heart with all diligence; for out of it are the issues of life.

## Proverbs 9:10-11

10 The fear of the Lord is the beginning of wisdom: and the knowledge of the holy is understanding.
11 For by me thy days shall be multiplied, and the years of thy life shall be increased.

## Proverbs 12:18

18 There is that speaketh like the piercings of a sword: but the tongue of the wise is health.

## Proverbs 13:17

17 A wicked messenger falleth into mischief: but a faithful ambassador is health.

## Proverbs 15:4

4 A wholesome tongue is a tree of life: but perverseness therein is a breach in the spirit.

## Proverbs 15:4

4 A wholesome tongue is a tree of life: but perverseness therein is a breach in the spirit.

## Proverbs 15:30

30 The light of the eyes rejoiceth the heart: and a good report maketh the bones fat.

## Proverbs 16:24

24 Pleasant words are as an honeycomb, sweet to the soul, and health to the bones.

## Proverbs 17:22

22 A merry heart doeth good like a medicine: but a broken spirit drieth the bones.

## Ecclesiastes 3:3

3 A time to kill, and a time to heal; a time to break down, and a time to build up;

## Ecclesiastes 5:17

17 All his days also he eateth in darkness, and he hath much sorrow and wrath with his sickness.

## Isaiah 6:10

[10] Make the heart of this people fat, and make their ears heavy, and shut their eyes; lest they see with their eyes, and hear with their ears, and understand with their heart, and convert, and be healed.

## Isaiah 19:22

[22] And the Lord shall smite Egypt: he shall smite and heal it: and they shall return even to the Lord, and he shall be intreated of them, and shall heal them.

## Isaiah 29:18

[18] And in that day shall the deaf hear the words of the book, and the eyes of the blind shall see out of obscurity, and out of darkness.

## Isaiah 30:26

[26] Moreover the light of the moon shall be as the light of the sun, and the light of the sun shall be sevenfold, as the light of seven days, in the day that the Lord bindeth up the breach of his people, and healeth the stroke of their wound.

## Isaiah 32:3-4

[3] And the eyes of them that see shall not be dim, and the ears of them that hear shall hearken.
[4] The heart also of the rash shall understand knowledge, and the tongue of the stammerers shall be ready to speak plainly.

## Isaiah 33:24

[24] And the inhabitant shall not say, I am sick: the people that dwell therein shall be forgiven their iniquity.

## Isaiah 35:5-6

5 Then the eyes of the blind shall be opened, and the ears of the deaf shall be unstopped.
6 Then shall the lame man leap as an hart, and the tongue of the dumb sing: for in the wilderness shall waters break out, and streams in the desert.

## Isaiah 38:16

16 O Lord, by these things men live, and in all these things is the life of my spirit: so wilt thou recover me, and make me to live.

## Isaiah 40:31

31 But they that wait upon the Lord shall renew their strength; they shall mount up with wings as eagles; they shall run, and not be weary; and they shall walk, and not faint.

## Isaiah 41:10

10 Fear thou not; for I am with thee: be not dismayed; for I am thy God: I will strengthen thee; yea, I will help thee; yea, I will uphold thee with the right hand of my righteousness.

## Isaiah 46:4

4 And even to your old age I am he; and even to hoar hairs will I carry you: I have made, and I will bear; even I will carry, and will deliver you.

## Isaiah 53:4-5

4 Surely he hath borne our griefs, and carried our sorrows: yet we did esteem him stricken, smitten of God, and afflicted.
5 But he was wounded for our transgressions, he was bruised for our iniquities: the chastisement of our peace was upon him; and with his stripes we are healed.

## Isaiah 57:18-19

[18] I have seen his ways, and will heal him: I will lead him also, and restore comforts unto him and to his mourners.
[19] I create the fruit of the lips; Peace, peace to him that is far off, and to him that is near, saith the Lord; and I will heal him.

## Isaiah 58:1-8

[1] Cry aloud, spare not, lift up thy voice like a trumpet, and shew my people their transgression, and the house of Jacob their sins.
[2] Yet they seek me daily, and delight to know my ways, as a nation that did righteousness, and forsook not the ordinance of their God: they ask of me the ordinances of justice; they take delight in approaching to God.
[3] Wherefore have we fasted, say they, and thou seest not? wherefore have we afflicted our soul, and thou takest no knowledge? Behold, in the day of your fast ye find pleasure, and exact all your labours.
[4] Behold, ye fast for strife and debate, and to smite with the fist of wickedness: ye shall not fast as ye do this day, to make your voice to be heard on high.
[5] Is it such a fast that I have chosen? a day for a man to afflict his soul? is it to bow down his head as a bulrush, and to spread sackcloth and ashes under him? wilt thou call this a fast, and an acceptable day to the Lord?
[6] Is not this the fast that I have chosen? to loose the bands of wickedness, to undo the heavy burdens, and to let the oppressed go free, and that ye break every yoke?
[7] Is it not to deal thy bread to the hungry, and that thou bring the poor that are cast out to thy house? when thou seest the naked, that thou cover him; and that thou hide not thyself from thine own flesh?
[8] Then shall thy light break forth as the morning, and thine health shall spring forth speedily: and thy righteousness

shall go before thee; the glory of the Lord shall be thy reward.

## Isaiah 61:1-3

[1] The Spirit of the Lord God is upon me; because the Lord hath anointed me to preach good tidings unto the meek; he hath sent me to bind up the brokenhearted, to proclaim liberty to the captives, and the opening of the prison to them that are bound;
[2] To proclaim the acceptable year of the Lord, and the day of vengeance of our God; to comfort all that mourn;
[3] To appoint unto them that mourn in Zion, to give unto them beauty for ashes, the oil of joy for mourning, the garment of praise for the spirit of heaviness; that they might be called trees of righteousness, the planting of the Lord, that he might be glorified.

## Jeremiah 3:22

[22] Return, ye backsliding children, and I will heal your backslidings. Behold, we come unto thee; for thou art the Lord our God.

## Jeremiah 6:14

[14] They have healed also the hurt of the daughter of my people slightly, saying, Peace, peace; when there is no peace.

## Jeremiah 8:11, 22

[11] They have healed also the hurt of the daughter of my people slightly, saying, Peace, peace; when there is no peace.

[22] Is there no balm in Gilead; is there no physician there? why then is not the health of the daughter of my people recovered?

## Jeremiah 8:14-15

[14] Why do we sit still? assemble yourselves, and let us enter into the defenced cities, and let us be silent there: for the Lord our God hath put us to silence, and given us water of gall to drink, because we have sinned against the Lord.
[15] We looked for peace, but no good came; and for a time of health, and behold trouble!

## Jeremiah 8:20-22

[20] The harvest is past, the summer is ended, and we are not saved.
[21] For the hurt of the daughter of my people am I hurt; I am black; astonishment hath taken hold on me.
[22] Is there no balm in Gilead; is there no physician there? why then is not the health of the daughter of my people recovered?

## Jeremiah 17:14

[14] Heal me, O Lord, and I shall be healed; save me, and I shall be saved: for thou art my praise.

## Jeremiah 30:12-17

[12] For thus saith the Lord, Thy bruise is incurable, and thy wound is grievous.
[13] There is none to plead thy cause, that thou mayest be bound up: thou hast no healing medicines.
[14] All thy lovers have forgotten thee; they seek thee not; for I have wounded thee with the wound of an enemy, with the chastisement of a cruel one, for the multitude of thine iniquity; because thy sins were increased.
[15] Why criest thou for thine affliction? thy sorrow is incurable for the multitude of thine iniquity: because thy sins were increased, I have done these things unto thee.
[16] Therefore all they that devour thee shall be devoured; and all thine adversaries, every one of them, shall go into

captivity; and they that spoil thee shall be a spoil, and all that prey upon thee will I give for a prey.
17 For I will restore health unto thee, and I will heal thee of thy wounds, saith the Lord; because they called thee an Outcast, saying, This is Zion, whom no man seeketh after.

## Jeremiah 33:6

6 Behold, I will bring it health and cure, and I will cure them, and will reveal unto them the abundance of peace and truth.

## Lamentations 3:33

33 For he doth not afflict willingly nor grieve the children of men.

## Ezekiel 34:16

16 I will seek that which was lost, and bring again that which was driven away, and will bind up that which was broken, and will strengthen that which was sick: but I will destroy the fat and the strong; I will feed them with judgment.

## Ezekiel 37:1-14

1 The hand of the Lord was upon me, and carried me out in the spirit of the Lord, and set me down in the midst of the valley which was full of bones,
2 And caused me to pass by them round about: and, behold, there were very many in the open valley; and, lo, they were very dry.
3 And he said unto me, Son of man, can these bones live? And I answered, O Lord God, thou knowest.
4 Again he said unto me, Prophesy upon these bones, and say unto them, O ye dry bones, hear the word of the Lord.
5 Thus saith the Lord God unto these bones; Behold, I will cause breath to enter into you, and ye shall live:

⁶ And I will lay sinews upon you, and will bring up flesh upon you, and cover you with skin, and put breath in you, and ye shall live; and ye shall know that I am the Lord.

⁷ So I prophesied as I was commanded: and as I prophesied, there was a noise, and behold a shaking, and the bones came together, bone to his bone.

⁸ And when I beheld, lo, the sinews and the flesh came up upon them, and the skin covered them above: but there was no breath in them.

⁹ Then said he unto me, Prophesy unto the wind, prophesy, son of man, and say to the wind, Thus saith the Lord God; Come from the four winds, O breath, and breathe upon these slain, that they may live.

¹⁰ So I prophesied as he commanded me, and the breath came into them, and they lived, and stood up upon their feet, an exceeding great army.

¹¹ Then he said unto me, Son of man, these bones are the whole house of Israel: behold, they say, Our bones are dried, and our hope is lost: we are cut off for our parts.

¹² Therefore prophesy and say unto them, Thus saith the Lord God; Behold, O my people, I will open your graves, and cause you to come up out of your graves, and bring you into the land of Israel.

¹³ And ye shall know that I am the Lord, when I have opened your graves, O my people, and brought you up out of your graves,

¹⁴ And shall put my spirit in you, and ye shall live, and I shall place you in your own land: then shall ye know that I the Lord have spoken it, and performed it, saith the Lord.

## Ezekiel 47:8-12

⁸ Then said he unto me, These waters issue out toward the east country, and go down into the desert, and go into the sea: which being brought forth into the sea, the waters shall be healed.

⁹ And it shall come to pass, that every thing that liveth, which moveth, whithersoever the rivers shall come, shall

live: and there shall be a very great multitude of fish, because these waters shall come thither: for they shall be healed; and every thing shall live whither the river cometh.
[10] And it shall come to pass, that the fishers shall stand upon it from Engedi even unto Eneglaim; they shall be a place to spread forth nets; their fish shall be according to their kinds, as the fish of the great sea, exceeding many.
[11] But the miry places thereof and the marishes thereof shall not be healed; they shall be given to salt.
[12] And by the river upon the bank thereof, on this side and on that side, shall grow all trees for meat, whose leaf shall not fade, neither shall the fruit thereof be consumed: it shall bring forth new fruit according to his months, because their waters they issued out of the sanctuary: and the fruit thereof shall be for meat, and the leaf thereof for medicine.

## Hosea 6:1-3

[1] Come, and let us return unto the Lord: for he hath torn, and he will heal us; he hath smitten, and he will bind us up.
[2] After two days will he revive us: in the third day he will raise us up, and we shall live in his sight.
[3] Then shall we know, if we follow on to know the Lord: his going forth is prepared as the morning; and he shall come unto us as the rain, as the latter and former rain unto the earth.

## Hosea 7:1

[1] When I would have healed Israel, then the iniquity of Ephraim was discovered, and the wickedness of Samaria: for they commit falsehood; and the thief cometh in, and the troop of robbers spoileth without.

## Hosea 14:4

[4] I will heal their backsliding, I will love them freely: for mine anger is turned away from him.

## Amos 5:4-6

4 For thus saith the Lord unto the house of Israel, Seek ye me, and ye shall live:
5 But seek not Bethel, nor enter into Gilgal, and pass not to Beersheba: for Gilgal shall surely go into captivity, and Bethel shall come to nought.
6 Seek the Lord, and ye shall live; lest he break out like fire in the house of Joseph, and devour it, and there be none to quench it in Bethel.

## Nahum 1:9

9 What do ye imagine against the Lord? he will make an utter end: affliction shall not rise up the second time.

## Malachi 4:2-3

2 But unto you that fear my name shall the Sun of righteousness arise with healing in his wings; and ye shall go forth, and grow up as calves of the stall.
3 And ye shall tread down the wicked; for they shall be ashes under the soles of your feet in the day that I shall do this, saith the Lord of hosts.

# *Healing Promises From The New Testament*

## Matthew 9:12-13

¹² But when Jesus heard that, he said unto them, They that be whole need not a physician, but they that are sick.
¹³ But go ye and learn what that meaneth, I will have mercy, and not sacrifice: for I am not come to call the righteous, but sinners to repentance.

## Matthew 10:1

¹ And when he had called unto him his twelve disciples, he gave them power against unclean spirits, to cast them out, and to heal all manner of sickness and all manner of disease.

## Matthew 10:7-8

⁷ And as ye go, preach, saying, The kingdom of heaven is at hand.
⁸ Heal the sick, cleanse the lepers, raise the dead, cast out devils: freely ye have received, freely give.

## Matthew 13:58

⁵⁸ And he did not many mighty works there because of their unbelief.

## Mark 16:17-18

¹⁷ And these signs shall follow them that believe; In my name shall they cast out devils; they shall speak with new tongues;

[18] They shall take up serpents; and if they drink any deadly thing, it shall not hurt them; they shall lay hands on the sick, and they shall recover.

## Luke 4:18-19

[18] The Spirit of the Lord is upon me, because he hath anointed me to preach the gospel to the poor; he hath sent me to heal the brokenhearted, to preach deliverance to the captives, and recovering of sight to the blind, to set at liberty them that are bruised,
[19] To preach the acceptable year of the Lord.

## Luke 5:17

[17] And it came to pass on a certain day, as he was teaching, that there were Pharisees and doctors of the law sitting by, which were come out of every town of Galilee, and Judaea, and Jerusalem: and the power of the Lord was present to heal them.

## Luke 9:1-2

[1] Then he called his twelve disciples together, and gave them power and authority over all devils, and to cure diseases.
[2] And he sent them to preach the kingdom of God, and to heal the sick.

## Luke 10:19

[19] Behold, I give unto you power to tread on serpents and scorpions, and over all the power of the enemy: and nothing shall by any means hurt you.

## John 14:12

[12] Verily, verily, I say unto you, He that believeth on me, the works that I do shall he do also; and greater works than these shall he do; because I go unto my Father.

## Acts 4:30

30 By stretching forth thine hand to heal; and that signs and wonders may be done by the name of thy holy child Jesus.

## Romans 8:11

11 But if the Spirit of him that raised up Jesus from the dead dwell in you, he that raised up Christ from the dead shall also quicken your mortal bodies by his Spirit that dwelleth in you.

## 1 Corinthians 12:7-11

7 But the manifestation of the Spirit is given to every man to profit withal.
8 For to one is given by the Spirit the word of wisdom; to another the word of knowledge by the same Spirit;
9 To another faith by the same Spirit; to another the gifts of healing by the same Spirit;
10 To another the working of miracles; to another prophecy; to another discerning of spirits; to another divers kinds of tongues; to another the interpretation of tongues:
11 But all these worketh that one and the selfsame Spirit, dividing to every man severally as he will.

## 1 Corinthians 12:27-31

27 Now ye are the body of Christ, and members in particular.
28 And God hath set some in the church, first apostles, secondarily prophets, thirdly teachers, after that miracles, then gifts of healings, helps, governments, diversities of tongues.
29 Are all apostles? are all prophets? are all teachers? are all workers of miracles?
30 Have all the gifts of healing? do all speak with tongues? do all interpret?
31 But covet earnestly the best gifts: and yet shew I unto you a more excellent way.

## James 5:13-16

[13] Is any among you afflicted? let him pray. Is any merry? let him sing psalms.
[14] Is any sick among you? let him call for the elders of the church; and let them pray over him, anointing him with oil in the name of the Lord:
[15] And the prayer of faith shall save the sick, and the Lord shall raise him up; and if he have committed sins, they shall be forgiven him.
[16] Confess your faults one to another, and pray one for another, that ye may be healed. The effectual fervent prayer of a righteous man availeth much.

## 1 Peter 2:24

[24] Who his own self bare our sins in his own body on the tree, that we, being dead to sins, should live unto righteousness: by whose stripes ye were healed.

## 3 John 1:2

[2] Beloved, I wish above all things that thou mayest prosper and be in health, even as thy soul prospereth.

# *Healing Examples From The Old Testament*

## 1. Abraham's Body Restored

### Genesis 15:2-6

2 And Abram said, Lord God, what wilt thou give me, seeing I go childless, and the steward of my house is this Eliezer of Damascus?
3 And Abram said, Behold, to me thou hast given no seed: and, lo, one born in my house is mine heir.
4 And, behold, the word of the Lord came unto him, saying, This shall not be thine heir; but he that shall come forth out of thine own bowels shall be thine heir.
5 And he brought him forth abroad, and said, Look now toward heaven, and tell the stars, if thou be able to number them: and he said unto him, So shall thy seed be.
6 And he believed in the Lord; and he counted it to him for righteousness.

## 2. Sarah's Womb Restored, Isaac Was Born

### Genesis 17:15-19; 18:10-14; 21:1-8

### Genesis 17:15-19

15 And God said unto Abraham, As for Sarai thy wife, thou shalt not call her name Sarai, but Sarah shall her name be.
16 And I will bless her, and give thee a son also of her: yea, I will bless her, and she shall be a mother of nations; kings of people shall be of her.

17 Then Abraham fell upon his face, and laughed, and said in his heart, Shall a child be born unto him that is an hundred years old? and shall Sarah, that is ninety years old, bear?
18 And Abraham said unto God, O that Ishmael might live before thee!
19 And God said, Sarah thy wife shall bear thee a son indeed; and thou shalt call his name Isaac: and I will establish my covenant with him for an everlasting covenant, and with his seed after him.

## Genesis 18:9-14

9 And they said unto him, Where is Sarah thy wife? And he said, Behold, in the tent.
10 And he said, I will certainly return unto thee according to the time of life; and, lo, Sarah thy wife shall have a son. And Sarah heard it in the tent door, which was behind him.
11 Now Abraham and Sarah were old and well stricken in age; and it ceased to be with Sarah after the manner of women.
12 Therefore Sarah laughed within herself, saying, After I am waxed old shall I have pleasure, my lord being old also?
13 And the Lord said unto Abraham, Wherefore did Sarah laugh, saying, Shall I of a surety bear a child, which am old?
14 Is any thing too hard for the Lord? At the time appointed I will return unto thee, according to the time of life, and Sarah shall have a son.

## Genesis 21:1-8

21 And the Lord visited Sarah as he had said, and the Lord did unto Sarah as he had spoken.
2 For Sarah conceived, and bare Abraham a son in his old age, at the set time of which God had spoken to him.
3 And Abraham called the name of his son that was born unto him, whom Sarah bare to him, Isaac.
4 And Abraham circumcised his son Isaac being eight days old, as God had commanded him.

Healing Examples From The Old Testament

5 And Abraham was an hundred years old, when his son Isaac was born unto him.
6 And Sarah said, God hath made me to laugh, so that all that hear will laugh with me.
7 And she said, Who would have said unto Abraham, that Sarah should have given children suck? for I have born him a son in his old age.
8 And the child grew, and was weaned: and Abraham made a great feast the same day that Isaac was weaned.

## 3. Abimelech, His Wife and Maidservants Healed (Abraham)

### Genesis 20:1-18

1 And Abraham journeyed from thence toward the south country, and dwelled between Kadesh and Shur, and sojourned in Gerar.
2 And Abraham said of Sarah his wife, She is my sister: and Abimelech king of Gerar sent, and took Sarah.
3 But God came to Abimelech in a dream by night, and said to him, Behold, thou art but a dead man, for the woman which thou hast taken; for she is a man's wife.
4 But Abimelech had not come near her: and he said, Lord, wilt thou slay also a righteous nation?
5 Said he not unto me, She is my sister? and she, even she herself said, He is my brother: in the integrity of my heart and innocency of my hands have I done this.
6 And God said unto him in a dream, Yea, I know that thou didst this in the integrity of thy heart; for I also withheld thee from sinning against me: therefore suffered I thee not to touch her.
7 Now therefore restore the man his wife; for he is a prophet, and he shall pray for thee, and thou shalt live: and if thou restore her not, know thou that thou shalt surely die, thou, and all that are thine.

## Healing Examples From The Old Testament

⁸ Therefore Abimelech rose early in the morning, and called all his servants, and told all these things in their ears: and the men were sore afraid.

⁹ Then Abimelech called Abraham, and said unto him, What hast thou done unto us? and what have I offended thee, that thou hast brought on me and on my kingdom a great sin? thou hast done deeds unto me that ought not to be done.

¹⁰ And Abimelech said unto Abraham, What sawest thou, that thou hast done this thing?

¹¹ And Abraham said, Because I thought, Surely the fear of God is not in this place; and they will slay me for my wife's sake.

¹² And yet indeed she is my sister; she is the daughter of my father, but not the daughter of my mother; and she became my wife.

¹³ And it came to pass, when God caused me to wander from my father's house, that I said unto her, This is thy kindness which thou shalt shew unto me; at every place whither we shall come, say of me, He is my brother.

¹⁴ And Abimelech took sheep, and oxen, and menservants, and womenservants, and gave them unto Abraham, and restored him Sarah his wife.

¹⁵ And Abimelech said, Behold, my land is before thee: dwell where it pleaseth thee.

¹⁶ And unto Sarah he said, Behold, I have given thy brother a thousand pieces of silver: behold, he is to thee a covering of the eyes, unto all that are with thee, and with all other: thus she was reproved.

¹⁷ So Abraham prayed unto God: and God healed Abimelech, and his wife, and his maidservants; and they bare children.

¹⁸ For the Lord had fast closed up all the wombs of the house of Abimelech, because of Sarah Abraham's wife.

Healing Examples From The Old Testament

## 4. Isaac Prayed, Rebekah's Womb Restored, Jacob and Esau Born

### Genesis 25:19-28

19 And these are the generations of Isaac, Abraham's son: Abraham begat Isaac:

20 And Isaac was forty years old when he took Rebekah to wife, the daughter of Bethuel the Syrian of Padanaram, the sister to Laban the Syrian.

21 And Isaac intreated the Lord for his wife, because she was barren: and the Lord was intreated of him, and Rebekah his wife conceived.

22 And the children struggled together within her; and she said, If it be so, why am I thus? And she went to enquire of the Lord.

23 And the Lord said unto her, Two nations are in thy womb, and two manner of people shall be separated from thy bowels; and the one people shall be stronger than the other people; and the elder shall serve the younger.

24 And when her days to be delivered were fulfilled, behold, there were twins in her womb.

25 And the first came out red, all over like an hairy garment; and they called his name Esau.

26 And after that came his brother out, and his hand took hold on Esau's heel; and his name was called Jacob: and Isaac was threescore years old when she bare them.

27 And the boys grew: and Esau was a cunning hunter, a man of the field; and Jacob was a plain man, dwelling in tents.

28 And Isaac loved Esau, because he did eat of his venison: but Rebekah loved Jacob.

## 5. Rachel's Womb Restored, Joseph Born

### Genesis 30:1-8, 22-24

¹ And when Rachel saw that she bare Jacob no children, Rachel envied her sister; and said unto Jacob, Give me children, or else I die.
² And Jacob's anger was kindled against Rachel: and he said, Am I in God's stead, who hath withheld from thee the fruit of the womb?

²² And God remembered Rachel, and God hearkened to her, and opened her womb.
²³ And she conceived, and bare a son; and said, God hath taken away my reproach:
²⁴ And she called his name Joseph; and said, The Lord shall add to me another son.

## 6. Moses Leprous Hand Restored

### Exodus 4:1-8

¹ And Moses answered and said, But, behold, they will not believe me, nor hearken unto my voice: for they will say, The Lord hath not appeared unto thee.
² And the Lord said unto him, What is that in thine hand? And he said, A rod.
³ And he said, Cast it on the ground. And he cast it on the ground, and it became a serpent; and Moses fled from before it.
⁴ And the Lord said unto Moses, Put forth thine hand, and take it by the tail. And he put forth his hand, and caught it, and it became a rod in his hand:
⁵ That they may believe that the Lord God of their fathers, the God of Abraham, the God of Isaac, and the God of Jacob, hath appeared unto thee.
⁶ And the Lord said furthermore unto him, Put now thine hand into thy bosom. And he put his hand into his bosom:

and when he took it out, behold, his hand was leprous as snow.
⁷ And he said, Put thine hand into thy bosom again. And he put his hand into his bosom again; and plucked it out of his bosom, and, behold, it was turned again as his other flesh.
⁸ And it shall come to pass, if they will not believe thee, neither hearken to the voice of the first sign, that they will believe the voice of the latter sign.

## 7.  Mariam Healed From Leprosy

### Numbers 12:1-15

¹ And Miriam and Aaron spake against Moses because of the Ethiopian woman whom he had married: for he had married an Ethiopian woman.
² And they said, Hath the Lord indeed spoken only by Moses? hath he not spoken also by us? And the Lord heard it.
³ (Now the man Moses was very meek, above all the men which were upon the face of the earth.)
⁴ And the Lord spake suddenly unto Moses, and unto Aaron, and unto Miriam, Come out ye three unto the tabernacle of the congregation. And they three came out.
⁵ And the Lord came down in the pillar of the cloud, and stood in the door of the tabernacle, and called Aaron and Miriam: and they both came forth.
⁶ And he said, Hear now my words: If there be a prophet among you, I the Lord will make myself known unto him in a vision, and will speak unto him in a dream.
⁷ My servant Moses is not so, who is faithful in all mine house.
⁸ With him will I speak mouth to mouth, even apparently, and not in dark speeches; and the similitude of the Lord shall he behold: wherefore then were ye not afraid to speak against my servant Moses?
⁹ And the anger of the Lord was kindled against them; and he departed.

10 And the cloud departed from off the tabernacle; and, behold, Miriam became leprous, white as snow: and Aaron looked upon Miriam, and, behold, she was leprous.
11 And Aaron said unto Moses, Alas, my lord, I beseech thee, lay not the sin upon us, wherein we have done foolishly, and wherein we have sinned.
12 Let her not be as one dead, of whom the flesh is half consumed when he cometh out of his mother's womb.
13 And Moses cried unto the Lord, saying, Heal her now, O God, I beseech thee.
14 And the Lord said unto Moses, If her father had but spit in her face, should she not be ashamed seven days? let her be shut out from the camp seven days, and after that let her be received in again.
15 And Miriam was shut out from the camp seven days: and the people journeyed not till Miriam was brought in again.

## 8. Aaron Stopped Plague Which Had Killed 14,700

### Numbers 16:41-50

41 But on the morrow all the congregation of the children of Israel murmured against Moses and against Aaron, saying, Ye have killed the people of the Lord.
42 And it came to pass, when the congregation was gathered against Moses and against Aaron, that they looked toward the tabernacle of the congregation: and, behold, the cloud covered it, and the glory of the Lord appeared.
43 And Moses and Aaron came before the tabernacle of the congregation.
44 And the Lord spake unto Moses, saying,
45 Get you up from among this congregation, that I may consume them as in a moment. And they fell upon their faces.
46 And Moses said unto Aaron, Take a censer, and put fire therein from off the altar, and put on incense, and go quickly

unto the congregation, and make an atonement for them: for there is wrath gone out from the Lord; the plague is begun.

[47] And Aaron took as Moses commanded, and ran into the midst of the congregation; and, behold, the plague was begun among the people: and he put on incense, and made an atonement for the people.

[48] And he stood between the dead and the living; and the plague was stayed.

[49] Now they that died in the plague were fourteen thousand and seven hundred, beside them that died about the matter of Korah.

[50] And Aaron returned unto Moses unto the door of the tabernacle of the congregation: and the plague was stayed.

## 9. Serpent of Brass Used to Heal From Snake Bites

### Numbers 21:4-9

[4] And they journeyed from mount Hor by the way of the Red sea, to compass the land of Edom: and the soul of the people was much discouraged because of the way.

[5] And the people spake against God, and against Moses, Wherefore have ye brought us up out of Egypt to die in the wilderness? for there is no bread, neither is there any water; and our soul loatheth this light bread.

[6] And the Lord sent fiery serpents among the people, and they bit the people; and much people of Israel died.

[7] Therefore the people came to Moses, and said, We have sinned, for we have spoken against the Lord, and against thee; pray unto the Lord, that he take away the serpents from us. And Moses prayed for the people.

[8] And the Lord said unto Moses, Make thee a fiery serpent, and set it upon a pole: and it shall come to pass, that every one that is bitten, when he looketh upon it, shall live.

[9] And Moses made a serpent of brass, and put it upon a pole, and it came to pass, that if a serpent had bitten any man, when he beheld the serpent of brass, he lived.

Healing Examples From The Old Testament

## 10. The Lord Sustained Joshua in the Dessert

### Joshua 14:10-11

10 And now, behold, the Lord hath kept me alive, as he said, these forty and five years, even since the Lord spake this word unto Moses, while the children of Israel wandered in the wilderness: and now, lo, I am this day fourscore and five years old.
11 As yet I am as strong this day as I was in the day that Moses sent me: as my strength was then, even so is my strength now, for war, both to go out, and to come in.

## 11. Manoah's Wife's Womb Restored, Samson Born

### Judges 13:1-25

1 And the children of Israel did evil again in the sight of the Lord; and the Lord delivered them into the hand of the Philistines forty years.
2 And there was a certain man of Zorah, of the family of the Danites, whose name was Manoah; and his wife was barren, and bare not.
3 And the angel of the Lord appeared unto the woman, and said unto her, Behold now, thou art barren, and bearest not: but thou shalt conceive, and bear a son.
4 Now therefore beware, I pray thee, and drink not wine nor strong drink, and eat not any unclean thing:
5 For, lo, thou shalt conceive, and bear a son; and no razor shall come on his head: for the child shall be a Nazarite unto God from the womb: and he shall begin to deliver Israel out of the hand of the Philistines.
6 Then the woman came and told her husband, saying, A man of God came unto me, and his countenance was like the countenance of an angel of God, very terrible: but I asked him not whence he was, neither told he me his name:

7 But he said unto me, Behold, thou shalt conceive, and bear a son; and now drink no wine nor strong drink, neither eat any unclean thing: for the child shall be a Nazarite to God from the womb to the day of his death.
8 Then Manoah intreated the Lord, and said, O my Lord, let the man of God which thou didst send come again unto us, and teach us what we shall do unto the child that shall be born.
9 And God hearkened to the voice of Manoah; and the angel of God came again unto the woman as she sat in the field: but Manoah her husband was not with her.
10 And the woman made haste, and ran, and shewed her husband, and said unto him, Behold, the man hath appeared unto me, that came unto me the other day.
11 And Manoah arose, and went after his wife, and came to the man, and said unto him, Art thou the man that spakest unto the woman? And he said, I am.
12 And Manoah said, Now let thy words come to pass. How shall we order the child, and how shall we do unto him?
13 And the angel of the Lord said unto Manoah, Of all that I said unto the woman let her beware.
14 She may not eat of any thing that cometh of the vine, neither let her drink wine or strong drink, nor eat any unclean thing: all that I commanded her let her observe.
15 And Manoah said unto the angel of the Lord, I pray thee, let us detain thee, until we shall have made ready a kid for thee.
16 And the angel of the Lord said unto Manoah, Though thou detain me, I will not eat of thy bread: and if thou wilt offer a burnt offering, thou must offer it unto the Lord. For Manoah knew not that he was an angel of the Lord.
17 And Manoah said unto the angel of the Lord, What is thy name, that when thy sayings come to pass we may do thee honour?
18 And the angel of the Lord said unto him, Why askest thou thus after my name, seeing it is secret?

Healing Examples From The Old Testament

19 So Manoah took a kid with a meat offering, and offered it upon a rock unto the Lord: and the angel did wonderously; and Manoah and his wife looked on.
20 For it came to pass, when the flame went up toward heaven from off the altar, that the angel of the Lord ascended in the flame of the altar. And Manoah and his wife looked on it, and fell on their faces to the ground.
21 But the angel of the Lord did no more appear to Manoah and to his wife. Then Manoah knew that he was an angel of the Lord.
22 And Manoah said unto his wife, We shall surely die, because we have seen God.
23 But his wife said unto him, If the Lord were pleased to kill us, he would not have received a burnt offering and a meat offering at our hands, neither would he have shewed us all these things, nor would as at this time have told us such things as these.
24 And the woman bare a son, and called his name Samson: and the child grew, and the Lord blessed him.
25 And the Spirit of the Lord began to move him at times in the camp of Dan between Zorah and Eshtaol.

## 12. Hannah's Womb Restored, Samuel Born

### I Samuel 1:1-20, 24; 2:18-21

### I Samuel 1:1-20, 24

1 Now there was a certain man of Ramathaimzophim, of mount Ephraim, and his name was Elkanah, the son of Jeroham, the son of Elihu, the son of Tohu, the son of Zuph, an Ephrathite:
2 And he had two wives; the name of the one was Hannah, and the name of the other Peninnah: and Peninnah had children, but Hannah had no children.
3 And this man went up out of his city yearly to worship and to sacrifice unto the Lord of hosts in Shiloh. And the two

sons of Eli, Hophni and Phinehas, the priests of the Lord, were there.
4 And when the time was that Elkanah offered, he gave to Peninnah his wife, and to all her sons and her daughters, portions:
5 But unto Hannah he gave a worthy portion; for he loved Hannah: but the Lord had shut up her womb.
6 And her adversary also provoked her sore, for to make her fret, because the Lord had shut up her womb.
7 And as he did so year by year, when she went up to the house of the Lord, so she provoked her; therefore she wept, and did not eat.
8 Then said Elkanah her husband to her, Hannah, why weepest thou? and why eatest thou not? and why is thy heart grieved? am not I better to thee than ten sons?
9 So Hannah rose up after they had eaten in Shiloh, and after they had drunk. Now Eli the priest sat upon a seat by a post of the temple of the Lord.
10 And she was in bitterness of soul, and prayed unto the Lord, and wept sore.
11 And she vowed a vow, and said, O Lord of hosts, if thou wilt indeed look on the affliction of thine handmaid, and remember me, and not forget thine handmaid, but wilt give unto thine handmaid a man child, then I will give him unto the Lord all the days of his life, and there shall no razor come upon his head.
12 And it came to pass, as she continued praying before the Lord, that Eli marked her mouth.
13 Now Hannah, she spake in her heart; only her lips moved, but her voice was not heard: therefore Eli thought she had been drunken.
14 And Eli said unto her, How long wilt thou be drunken? put away thy wine from thee.
15 And Hannah answered and said, No, my lord, I am a woman of a sorrowful spirit: I have drunk neither wine nor strong drink, but have poured out my soul before the Lord.

16 Count not thine handmaid for a daughter of Belial: for out of the abundance of my complaint and grief have I spoken hitherto.
17 Then Eli answered and said, Go in peace: and the God of Israel grant thee thy petition that thou hast asked of him.
18 And she said, Let thine handmaid find grace in thy sight. So the woman went her way, and did eat, and her countenance was no more sad.
19 And they rose up in the morning early, and worshipped before the Lord, and returned, and came to their house to Ramah: and Elkanah knew Hannah his wife; and the Lord remembered her.
20 Wherefore it came to pass, when the time was come about after Hannah had conceived, that she bare a son, and called his name Samuel, saying, Because I have asked him of the Lord.

24 And when she had weaned him, she took him up with her, with three bullocks, and one ephah of flour, and a bottle of wine, and brought him unto the house of the Lord in Shiloh: and the child was young.

**I Samuel 2:18-21**

18 But Samuel ministered before the Lord, being a child, girded with a linen ephod.
19 Moreover his mother made him a little coat, and brought it to him from year to year, when she came up with her husband to offer the yearly sacrifice.
20 And Eli blessed Elkanah and his wife, and said, The Lord give thee seed of this woman for the loan which is lent to the Lord. And they went unto their own home.
21 And the Lord visited Hannah, so that she conceived, and bare three sons and two daughters. And the child Samuel grew before the Lord.

## 13. Return of Ark Brings Healing for Philistines

### I Samuel 6:3

3 And they said, If ye send away the ark of the God of Israel, send it not empty; but in any wise return him a trespass offering: then ye shall be healed, and it shall be known to you why his hand is not removed from you.

## 14. David Sinned – Plagued Stopped After 70,000 Die

### 2 Samuel 24:10-25

10 And David's heart smote him after that he had numbered the people. And David said unto the Lord, I have sinned greatly in that I have done: and now, I beseech thee, O Lord, take away the iniquity of thy servant; for I have done very foolishly.
11 For when David was up in the morning, the word of the Lord came unto the prophet Gad, David's seer, saying,
12 Go and say unto David, Thus saith the Lord, I offer thee three things; choose thee one of them, that I may do it unto thee.
13 So Gad came to David, and told him, and said unto him, Shall seven years of famine come unto thee in thy land? or wilt thou flee three months before thine enemies, while they pursue thee? or that there be three days' pestilence in thy land? now advise, and see what answer I shall return to him that sent me.
14 And David said unto Gad, I am in a great strait: let us fall now into the hand of the Lord; for his mercies are great: and let me not fall into the hand of man.
15 So the Lord sent a pestilence upon Israel from the morning even to the time appointed: and there died of the people from Dan even to Beersheba seventy thousand men.
16 And when the angel stretched out his hand upon Jerusalem to destroy it, the Lord repented him of the evil, and said to the angel that destroyed the people, It is enough:

stay now thine hand. And the angel of the Lord was by the threshingplace of Araunah the Jebusite.

17 And David spake unto the Lord when he saw the angel that smote the people, and said, Lo, I have sinned, and I have done wickedly: but these sheep, what have they done? let thine hand, I pray thee, be against me, and against my father's house.

18 And Gad came that day to David, and said unto him, Go up, rear an altar unto the Lord in the threshingfloor of Araunah the Jebusite.

19 And David, according to the saying of Gad, went up as the Lord commanded.

20 And Araunah looked, and saw the king and his servants coming on toward him: and Araunah went out, and bowed himself before the king on his face upon the ground.

21 And Araunah said, Wherefore is my lord the king come to his servant? And David said, To buy the threshingfloor of thee, to build an altar unto the Lord, that the plague may be stayed from the people.

22 And Araunah said unto David, Let my lord the king take and offer up what seemeth good unto him: behold, here be oxen for burnt sacrifice, and threshing instruments and other instruments of the oxen for wood.

23 All these things did Araunah, as a king, give unto the king. And Araunah said unto the king, The Lord thy God accept thee.

24 And the king said unto Araunah, Nay; but I will surely buy it of thee at a price: neither will I offer burnt offerings unto the Lord my God of that which doth cost me nothing. So David bought the threshingfloor and the oxen for fifty shekels of silver.

25 And David built there an altar unto the Lord, and offered burnt offerings and peace offerings. So the Lord was intreated for the land, and the plague was stayed from Israel.

Healing Examples From The Old Testament

## 15. King Jeroboam's Withered Hand Restored

### I Kings 13:1-10

[1] And, behold, there came a man of God out of Judah by the word of the Lord unto Bethel: and Jeroboam stood by the altar to burn incense.
[2] And he cried against the altar in the word of the Lord, and said, O altar, altar, thus saith the Lord; Behold, a child shall be born unto the house of David, Josiah by name; and upon thee shall he offer the priests of the high places that burn incense upon thee, and men's bones shall be burnt upon thee.
[3] And he gave a sign the same day, saying, This is the sign which the Lord hath spoken; Behold, the altar shall be rent, and the ashes that are upon it shall be poured out.
[4] And it came to pass, when king Jeroboam heard the saying of the man of God, which had cried against the altar in Bethel, that he put forth his hand from the altar, saying, Lay hold on him. And his hand, which he put forth against him, dried up, so that he could not pull it in again to him.
[5] The altar also was rent, and the ashes poured out from the altar, according to the sign which the man of God had given by the word of the Lord.
[6] And the king answered and said unto the man of God, Intreat now the face of the Lord thy God, and pray for me, that my hand may be restored me again. And the man of God besought the Lord, and the king's hand was restored him again, and became as it was before.
[7] And the king said unto the man of God, Come home with me, and refresh thyself, and I will give thee a reward.
[8] And the man of God said unto the king, If thou wilt give me half thine house, I will not go in with thee, neither will I eat bread nor drink water in this place:
[9] For so was it charged me by the word of the Lord, saying, Eat no bread, nor drink water, nor turn again by the same way that thou camest.

10 So he went another way, and returned not by the way that he came to Bethel

## 16. Son of the Widow of Zarephath Brought Back to Life (Elijah)

### I Kings 17:17-24

17 And it came to pass after these things, that the son of the woman, the mistress of the house, fell sick; and his sickness was so sore, that there was no breath left in him.
18 And she said unto Elijah, What have I to do with thee, O thou man of God? art thou come unto me to call my sin to remembrance, and to slay my son?
19 And he said unto her, Give me thy son. And he took him out of her bosom, and carried him up into a loft, where he abode, and laid him upon his own bed.
20 And he cried unto the Lord, and said, O Lord my God, hast thou also brought evil upon the widow with whom I sojourn, by slaying her son?
21 And he stretched himself upon the child three times, and cried unto the Lord, and said, O Lord my God, I pray thee, let this child's soul come into him again.
22 And the Lord heard the voice of Elijah; and the soul of the child came into him again, and he revived.
23 And Elijah took the child, and brought him down out of the chamber into the house, and delivered him unto his mother: and Elijah said, See, thy son liveth.
24 And the woman said to Elijah, Now by this I know that thou art a man of God, and that the word of the Lord in thy mouth is truth.

## 17. King Ahaziah Did Not Get Healed

### II Kings 1:1-4, 15-17

1 Then Moab rebelled against Israel after the death of Ahab.

## Healing Examples From The Old Testament

2 And Ahaziah fell down through a lattice in his upper chamber that was in Samaria, and was sick: and he sent messengers, and said unto them, Go, enquire of Baalzebub the god of Ekron whether I shall recover of this disease.
3 But the angel of the Lord said to Elijah the Tishbite, Arise, go up to meet the messengers of the king of Samaria, and say unto them, Is it not because there is not a God in Israel, that ye go to enquire of Baalzebub the god of Ekron?
4 Now therefore thus saith the Lord, Thou shalt not come down from that bed on which thou art gone up, but shalt surely die. And Elijah departed.

15 And the angel of the Lord said unto Elijah, Go down with him: be not afraid of him. And he arose, and went down with him unto the king.
16 And he said unto him, Thus saith the Lord, Forasmuch as thou hast sent messengers to enquire of Baalzebub the god of Ekron, is it not because there is no God in Israel to enquire of his word? therefore thou shalt not come down off that bed on which thou art gone up, but shalt surely die.
17 So he died according to the word of the Lord which Elijah had spoken. And Jehoram reigned in his stead in the second year of Jehoram the son of Jehoshaphat king of Judah; because he had no son.

## 18. Water Healed (Elisha)

### II Kings 2:19-22

19 And the men of the city said unto Elisha, Behold, I pray thee, the situation of this city is pleasant, as my lord seeth: but the water is naught, and the ground barren.
20 And he said, Bring me a new cruse, and put salt therein. And they brought it to him.
21 And he went forth unto the spring of the waters, and cast the salt in there, and said, Thus saith the Lord, I have

healed these waters; there shall not be from thence any more death or barren land.

22 So the waters were healed unto this day, according to the saying of Elisha which he spake.

# 19. Shunammite Woman's Womb Restored, Son Born (Elisha)

## II Kings 4:8-17

8 And it fell on a day, that Elisha passed to Shunem, where was a great woman; and she constrained him to eat bread. And so it was, that as oft as he passed by, he turned in thither to eat bread.

9 And she said unto her husband, Behold now, I perceive that this is an holy man of God, which passeth by us continually.

10 Let us make a little chamber, I pray thee, on the wall; and let us set for him there a bed, and a table, and a stool, and a candlestick: and it shall be, when he cometh to us, that he shall turn in thither.

11 And it fell on a day, that he came thither, and he turned into the chamber, and lay there.

12 And he said to Gehazi his servant, Call this Shunammite. And when he had called her, she stood before him.

13 And he said unto him, Say now unto her, Behold, thou hast been careful for us with all this care; what is to be done for thee? wouldest thou be spoken for to the king, or to the captain of the host? And she answered, I dwell among mine own people.

14 And he said, What then is to be done for her? And Gehazi answered, Verily she hath no child, and her husband is old.

15 And he said, Call her. And when he had called her, she stood in the door.

16 And he said, About this season, according to the time of life, thou shalt embrace a son. And she said, Nay, my lord, thou man of God, do not lie unto thine handmaid.

Healing Examples From The Old Testament

17 And the woman conceived, and bare a son at that season that Elisha had said unto her, according to the time of life.

## 20. Shunammite Woman's Son Raised From The Dead (Elisha)

### II Kings 4:18-37

18 And when the child was grown, it fell on a day, that he went out to his father to the reapers.

19 And he said unto his father, My head, my head. And he said to a lad, Carry him to his mother.

20 And when he had taken him, and brought him to his mother, he sat on her knees till noon, and then died.

21 And she went up, and laid him on the bed of the man of God, and shut the door upon him, and went out.

22 And she called unto her husband, and said, Send me, I pray thee, one of the young men, and one of the asses, that I may run to the man of God, and come again.

23 And he said, Wherefore wilt thou go to him to day? it is neither new moon, nor sabbath. And she said, It shall be well.

24 Then she saddled an ass, and said to her servant, Drive, and go forward; slack not thy riding for me, except I bid thee.

25 So she went and came unto the man of God to mount Carmel. And it came to pass, when the man of God saw her afar off, that he said to Gehazi his servant, Behold, yonder is that Shunammite:

26 Run now, I pray thee, to meet her, and say unto her, Is it well with thee? is it well with thy husband? is it well with the child? And she answered, It is well:

27 And when she came to the man of God to the hill, she caught him by the feet: but Gehazi came near to thrust her away. And the man of God said, Let her alone; for her soul is vexed within her: and the Lord hath hid it from me, and hath not told me.

28 Then she said, Did I desire a son of my lord? did I not say, Do not deceive me?
29 Then he said to Gehazi, Gird up thy loins, and take my staff in thine hand, and go thy way: if thou meet any man, salute him not; and if any salute thee, answer him not again: and lay my staff upon the face of the child.
30 And the mother of the child said, As the Lord liveth, and as thy soul liveth, I will not leave thee. And he arose, and followed her.
31 And Gehazi passed on before them, and laid the staff upon the face of the child; but there was neither voice, nor hearing. Wherefore he went again to meet him, and told him, saying, The child is not awaked.
32 And when Elisha was come into the house, behold, the child was dead, and laid upon his bed.
33 He went in therefore, and shut the door upon them twain, and prayed unto the Lord.
34 And he went up, and lay upon the child, and put his mouth upon his mouth, and his eyes upon his eyes, and his hands upon his hands: and stretched himself upon the child; and the flesh of the child waxed warm.
35 Then he returned, and walked in the house to and fro; and went up, and stretched himself upon him: and the child sneezed seven times, and the child opened his eyes.
36 And he called Gehazi, and said, Call this Shunammite. So he called her. And when she was come in unto him, he said, Take up thy son.
37 Then she went in, and fell at his feet, and bowed herself to the ground, and took up her son, and went out.

## 21. Healing for Death in the Pot (Elisha)

### II Kings 4:41

38 And Elisha came again to Gilgal: and there was a dearth in the land; and the sons of the prophets were sitting before

him: and he said unto his servant, Set on the great pot, and seethe pottage for the sons of the prophets.

39 And one went out into the field to gather herbs, and found a wild vine, and gathered thereof wild gourds his lap full, and came and shred them into the pot of pottage: for they knew them not.

40 So they poured out for the men to eat. And it came to pass, as they were eating of the pottage, that they cried out, and said, O thou man of God, there is death in the pot. And they could not eat thereof.

41 But he said, Then bring meal. And he cast it into the pot; and he said, Pour out for the people, that they may eat. And there was no harm in the pot.

## 22. Naaman Cleansed of Leprosy (Elisha)

### II Kings 5:1-15

5 Now Naaman, captain of the host of the king of Syria, was a great man with his master, and honourable, because by him the Lord had given deliverance unto Syria: he was also a mighty man in valour, but he was a leper.

2 And the Syrians had gone out by companies, and had brought away captive out of the land of Israel a little maid; and she waited on Naaman's wife.

3 And she said unto her mistress, Would God my lord were with the prophet that is in Samaria! for he would recover him of his leprosy.

4 And one went in, and told his lord, saying, Thus and thus said the maid that is of the land of Israel.

5 And the king of Syria said, Go to, go, and I will send a letter unto the king of Israel. And he departed, and took with him ten talents of silver, and six thousand pieces of gold, and ten changes of raiment.

6 And he brought the letter to the king of Israel, saying, Now when this letter is come unto thee, behold, I have therewith

sent Naaman my servant to thee, that thou mayest recover him of his leprosy.

⁷ And it came to pass, when the king of Israel had read the letter, that he rent his clothes, and said, Am I God, to kill and to make alive, that this man doth send unto me to recover a man of his leprosy? wherefore consider, I pray you, and see how he seeketh a quarrel against me.

⁸ And it was so, when Elisha the man of God had heard that the king of Israel had rent his clothes, that he sent to the king, saying, Wherefore hast thou rent thy clothes? let him come now to me, and he shall know that there is a prophet in Israel.

⁹ So Naaman came with his horses and with his chariot, and stood at the door of the house of Elisha.

¹⁰ And Elisha sent a messenger unto him, saying, Go and wash in Jordan seven times, and thy flesh shall come again to thee, and thou shalt be clean.

¹¹ But Naaman was wroth, and went away, and said, Behold, I thought, He will surely come out to me, and stand, and call on the name of the Lord his God, and strike his hand over the place, and recover the leper.

¹² Are not Abana and Pharpar, rivers of Damascus, better than all the waters of Israel? may I not wash in them, and be clean? So he turned and went away in a rage.

¹³ And his servants came near, and spake unto him, and said, My father, if the prophet had bid thee do some great thing, wouldest thou not have done it? how much rather then, when he saith to thee, Wash, and be clean?

¹⁴ Then went he down, and dipped himself seven times in Jordan, according to the saying of the man of God: and his flesh came again like unto the flesh of a little child, and he was clean.

¹⁵ And he returned to the man of God, he and all his company, and came, and stood before him: and he said, Behold, now I know that there is no God in all the earth, but in Israel: now therefore, I pray thee, take a blessing of thy servant.

Healing Examples From The Old Testament

## 23. Dead Man Revived in Elisha's Tomb

### II Kings 13:14, 21

[20] And Elisha died, and they buried him. And the bands of the Moabites invaded the land at the coming in of the year.
[21] And it came to pass, as they were burying a man, that, behold, they spied a band of men; and they cast the man into the sepulchre of Elisha: and when the man was let down, and touched the bones of Elisha, he revived, and stood up on his feet.

## 24. Terminally Ill King Hezekiah Had 15 Years Added to His Life (Isaiah)

### II Kings 20:1-11, II Chronicles 32:24-26, Isaiah 38:1-(8)22

### II Kings 20:1-11

[1] In those days was Hezekiah sick unto death. And the prophet Isaiah the son of Amoz came to him, and said unto him, Thus saith the Lord, Set thine house in order; for thou shalt die, and not live.
[2] Then he turned his face to the wall, and prayed unto the Lord, saying,
[3] I beseech thee, O Lord, remember now how I have walked before thee in truth and with a perfect heart, and have done that which is good in thy sight. And Hezekiah wept sore.
[4] And it came to pass, afore Isaiah was gone out into the middle court, that the word of the Lord came to him, saying,
[5] Turn again, and tell Hezekiah the captain of my people, Thus saith the Lord, the God of David thy father, I have heard thy prayer, I have seen thy tears: behold, I will heal thee: on the third day thou shalt go up unto the house of the Lord.

## Healing Examples From The Old Testament

⁶ And I will add unto thy days fifteen years; and I will deliver thee and this city out of the hand of the king of Assyria; and I will defend this city for mine own sake, and for my servant David's sake.

⁷ And Isaiah said, Take a lump of figs. And they took and laid it on the boil, and he recovered.

⁸ And Hezekiah said unto Isaiah, What shall be the sign that the Lord will heal me, and that I shall go up into the house of the Lord the third day?

⁹ And Isaiah said, This sign shalt thou have of the Lord, that the Lord will do the thing that he hath spoken: shall the shadow go forward ten degrees, or go back ten degrees?

¹⁰ And Hezekiah answered, It is a light thing for the shadow to go down ten degrees: nay, but let the shadow return backward ten degrees.

¹¹ And Isaiah the prophet cried unto the Lord: and he brought the shadow ten degrees backward, by which it had gone down in the dial of Ahaz.

## II Chronicles 32:24-26

²⁴ In those days Hezekiah was sick to the death, and prayed unto the Lord: and he spake unto him, and he gave him a sign.

²⁵ But Hezekiah rendered not again according to the benefit done unto him; for his heart was lifted up: therefore there was wrath upon him, and upon Judah and Jerusalem.

²⁶ Notwithstanding Hezekiah humbled himself for the pride of his heart, both he and the inhabitants of Jerusalem, so that the wrath of the Lord came not upon them in the days of Hezekiah.

## Isaiah 38:1-22

¹ In those days was Hezekiah sick unto death. And Isaiah the prophet the son of Amoz came unto him, and said unto him, Thus saith the Lord, Set thine house in order: for thou shalt die, and not live.

2 Then Hezekiah turned his face toward the wall, and prayed unto the Lord,
3 And said, Remember now, O Lord, I beseech thee, how I have walked before thee in truth and with a perfect heart, and have done that which is good in thy sight. And Hezekiah wept sore.
4 Then came the word of the Lord to Isaiah, saying,
5 Go, and say to Hezekiah, Thus saith the Lord, the God of David thy father, I have heard thy prayer, I have seen thy tears: behold, I will add unto thy days fifteen years.
6 And I will deliver thee and this city out of the hand of the king of Assyria: and I will defend this city.
7 And this shall be a sign unto thee from the Lord, that the Lord will do this thing that he hath spoken;
8 Behold, I will bring again the shadow of the degrees, which is gone down in the sun dial of Ahaz, ten degrees backward. So the sun returned ten degrees, by which degrees it was gone down.
9 The writing of Hezekiah king of Judah, when he had been sick, and was recovered of his sickness:
10 I said in the cutting off of my days, I shall go to the gates of the grave: I am deprived of the residue of my years.
11 I said, I shall not see the Lord, even the Lord, in the land of the living: I shall behold man no more with the inhabitants of the world.
12 Mine age is departed, and is removed from me as a shepherd's tent: I have cut off like a weaver my life: he will cut me off with pining sickness: from day even to night wilt thou make an end of me.
13 I reckoned till morning, that, as a lion, so will he break all my bones: from day even to night wilt thou make an end of me.
14 Like a crane or a swallow, so did I chatter: I did mourn as a dove: mine eyes fail with looking upward: O Lord, I am oppressed; undertake for me.

Healing Examples From The Old Testament

15 What shall I say? he hath both spoken unto me, and himself hath done it: I shall go softly all my years in the bitterness of my soul.

16 O Lord, by these things men live, and in all these things is the life of my spirit: so wilt thou recover me, and make me to live.

17 Behold, for peace I had great bitterness: but thou hast in love to my soul delivered it from the pit of corruption: for thou hast cast all my sins behind thy back.

18 For the grave cannot praise thee, death can not celebrate thee: they that go down into the pit cannot hope for thy truth.

19 The living, the living, he shall praise thee, as I do this day: the father to the children shall make known thy truth.

20 The Lord was ready to save me: therefore we will sing my songs to the stringed instruments all the days of our life in the house of the Lord.

21 For Isaiah had said, Let them take a lump of figs, and lay it for a plaister upon the boil, and he shall recover.

22 Hezekiah also had said, What is the sign that I shall go up to the house of the Lord?

## 25. King Asa Ignored God – Did Not Get Healed

### II Chronicles 6:12-13

12 And Asa in the thirty and ninth year of his reign was diseased in his feet, until his disease was exceeding great: yet in his disease he sought not to the Lord, but to the physicians.

13 And Asa slept with his fathers, and died in the one and fortieth year of his reign.

Healing Examples From The Old Testament

## 26. King Uzziah's Sin Caused Leprosy

### II Chronicles 26:16-31

16 But when he was strong, his heart was lifted up to his destruction: for he transgressed against the Lord his God, and went into the temple of the Lord to burn incense upon the altar of incense.

17 And Azariah the priest went in after him, and with him fourscore priests of the Lord, that were valiant men:

18 And they withstood Uzziah the king, and said unto him, It appertaineth not unto thee, Uzziah, to burn incense unto the Lord, but to the priests the sons of Aaron, that are consecrated to burn incense: go out of the sanctuary; for thou hast trespassed; neither shall it be for thine honour from the Lord God.

19 Then Uzziah was wroth, and had a censer in his hand to burn incense: and while he was wroth with the priests, the leprosy even rose up in his forehead before the priests in the house of the Lord, from beside the incense altar.

20 And Azariah the chief priest, and all the priests, looked upon him, and, behold, he was leprous in his forehead, and they thrust him out from thence; yea, himself hasted also to go out, because the Lord had smitten him.

21 And Uzziah the king was a leper unto the day of his death, and dwelt in a several house, being a leper; for he was cut off from the house of the Lord: and Jotham his son was over the king's house, judging the people of the land.

22 Now the rest of the acts of Uzziah, first and last, did Isaiah the prophet, the son of Amoz, write.

23 So Uzziah slept with his fathers, and they buried him with his fathers in the field of the burial which belonged to the kings; for they said, He is a leper: and Jotham his son reigned in his stead.

Healing Examples From The Old Testament

## 27. King Hezekiah Prayed for Israel's Healing

### II Chronicles 30:15-20

15 Then they killed the passover on the fourteenth day of the second month: and the priests and the Levites were ashamed, and sanctified themselves, and brought in the burnt offerings into the house of the Lord.
16 And they stood in their place after their manner, according to the law of Moses the man of God: the priests sprinkled the blood, which they received of the hand of the Levites.
17 For there were many in the congregation that were not sanctified: therefore the Levites had the charge of the killing of the passovers for every one that was not clean, to sanctify them unto the Lord.
18 For a multitude of the people, even many of Ephraim, and Manasseh, Issachar, and Zebulun, had not cleansed themselves, yet did they eat the passover otherwise than it was written. But Hezekiah prayed for them, saying, The good Lord pardon every one
19 That prepareth his heart to seek God, the Lord God of his fathers, though he be not cleansed according to the purification of the sanctuary.
20 And the Lord hearkened to Hezekiah, and healed the people.

## 28. Job Repented and Prayed for His Friends, He Was Restored

### Job 42:1-17

1 Then Job answered the Lord, and said,
2 I know that thou canst do every thing, and that no thought can be withholden from thee.
3 Who is he that hideth counsel without knowledge? therefore have I uttered that I understood not; things too wonderful for me, which I knew not.

## Healing Examples From The Old Testament

⁴ Hear, I beseech thee, and I will speak: I will demand of thee, and declare thou unto me.
⁵ I have heard of thee by the hearing of the ear: but now mine eye seeth thee.
⁶ Wherefore I abhor myself, and repent in dust and ashes.
⁷ And it was so, that after the Lord had spoken these words unto Job, the Lord said to Eliphaz the Temanite, My wrath is kindled against thee, and against thy two friends: for ye have not spoken of me the thing that is right, as my servant Job hath.
⁸ Therefore take unto you now seven bullocks and seven rams, and go to my servant Job, and offer up for yourselves a burnt offering; and my servant Job shall pray for you: for him will I accept: lest I deal with you after your folly, in that ye have not spoken of me the thing which is right, like my servant Job.
⁹ So Eliphaz the Temanite and Bildad the Shuhite and Zophar the Naamathite went, and did according as the Lord commanded them: the Lord also accepted Job.
¹⁰ And the Lord turned the captivity of Job, when he prayed for his friends: also the Lord gave Job twice as much as he had before.
¹¹ Then came there unto him all his brethren, and all his sisters, and all they that had been of his acquaintance before, and did eat bread with him in his house: and they bemoaned him, and comforted him over all the evil that the Lord had brought upon him: every man also gave him a piece of money, and every one an earring of gold.
¹² So the Lord blessed the latter end of Job more than his beginning: for he had fourteen thousand sheep, and six thousand camels, and a thousand yoke of oxen, and a thousand she asses.
¹³ He had also seven sons and three daughters.
¹⁴ And he called the name of the first, Jemima; and the name of the second, Kezia; and the name of the third, Kerenhappuch.

Healing Examples From The Old Testament

15 And in all the land were no women found so fair as the daughters of Job: and their father gave them inheritance among their brethren.
16 After this lived Job an hundred and forty years, and saw his sons, and his sons' sons, even four generations.
17 So Job died, being old and full of days.

## 29. David Healed

### Psalms 30:2-3

2 O Lord my God, I cried unto thee, and thou hast healed me.
3 O Lord, thou hast brought up my soul from the grave: thou hast kept me alive, that I should not go down to the pit.

## 30. Nebuchadnezzar Punished With Insanity, Then Healed

### Daniel 4:29-37

29 At the end of twelve months he walked in the palace of the kingdom of Babylon.
30 The king spake, and said, Is not this great Babylon, that I have built for the house of the kingdom by the might of my power, and for the honour of my majesty?
31 While the word was in the king's mouth, there fell a voice from heaven, saying, O king Nebuchadnezzar, to thee it is spoken; The kingdom is departed from thee.
32 And they shall drive thee from men, and thy dwelling shall be with the beasts of the field: they shall make thee to eat grass as oxen, and seven times shall pass over thee, until thou know that the most High ruleth in the kingdom of men, and giveth it to whomsoever he will.
33 The same hour was the thing fulfilled upon Nebuchadnezzar: and he was driven from men, and did eat grass as oxen, and his body was wet with the dew of heaven,

till his hairs were grown like eagles' feathers, and his nails like birds' claws.

34 And at the end of the days I Nebuchadnezzar lifted up mine eyes unto heaven, and mine understanding returned unto me, and I blessed the most High, and I praised and honoured him that liveth for ever, whose dominion is an everlasting dominion, and his kingdom is from generation to generation:

35 And all the inhabitants of the earth are reputed as nothing: and he doeth according to his will in the army of heaven, and among the inhabitants of the earth: and none can stay his hand, or say unto him, What doest thou?

36 At the same time my reason returned unto me; and for the glory of my kingdom, mine honour and brightness returned unto me; and my counsellors and my lords sought unto me; and I was established in my kingdom, and excellent majesty was added unto me.

37 Now I Nebuchadnezzar praise and extol and honour the King of heaven, all whose works are truth, and his ways judgment: and those that walk in pride he is able to abase.

## 31. Israel Healed

### Hosea 11:1-3

1 When Israel was a child, then I loved him, and called my son out of Egypt.

2 As they called them, so they went from them: they sacrificed unto Baalim, and burned incense to graven images.

3 I taught Ephraim also to go, taking them by their arms; but they knew not that I healed them.

# *Healing Examples From The New Testament: The Gospels*

## 1. Jesus Teaches, Preaches and Heals In Synagogues in Galilee

### Matthew 4:23-25; 4:12-25; Mark 1:35-39; Luke 4:42-44

**Matthew 4:23-25**

23 And Jesus went about all Galilee, teaching in their synagogues, and preaching the gospel of the kingdom, and healing all manner of sickness and all manner of disease among the people.
24 And his fame went throughout all Syria: and they brought unto him all sick people that were taken with divers diseases and torments, and those which were possessed with devils, and those which were lunatick, and those that had the palsy; and he healed them.
25 And there followed him great multitudes of people from Galilee, and from Decapolis, and from Jerusalem, and from Judaea, and from beyond Jordan.

**Matthew 4:12-25**

12 Now when Jesus had heard that John was cast into prison, he departed into Galilee;
13 And leaving Nazareth, he came and dwelt in Capernaum, which is upon the sea coast, in the borders of Zabulon and Nephthalim:

¹⁴ That it might be fulfilled which was spoken by Esaias the prophet, saying,
¹⁵ The land of Zabulon, and the land of Nephthalim, by the way of the sea, beyond Jordan, Galilee of the Gentiles;
¹⁶ The people which sat in darkness saw great light; and to them which sat in the region and shadow of death light is sprung up.
¹⁷ From that time Jesus began to preach, and to say, Repent: for the kingdom of heaven is at hand.
¹⁸ And Jesus, walking by the sea of Galilee, saw two brethren, Simon called Peter, and Andrew his brother, casting a net into the sea: for they were fishers.
¹⁹ And he saith unto them, Follow me, and I will make you fishers of men.
²⁰ And they straightway left their nets, and followed him.
²¹ And going on from thence, he saw other two brethren, James the son of Zebedee, and John his brother, in a ship with Zebedee their father, mending their nets; and he called them.
²² And they immediately left the ship and their father, and followed him.
²³ And Jesus went about all Galilee, teaching in their synagogues, and preaching the gospel of the kingdom, and healing all manner of sickness and all manner of disease among the people.
²⁴ And his fame went throughout all Syria: and they brought unto him all sick people that were taken with divers diseases and torments, and those which were possessed with devils, and those which were lunatick, and those that had the palsy; and he healed them.
²⁵ And there followed him great multitudes of people from Galilee, and from Decapolis, and from Jerusalem, and from Judaea, and from beyond Jordan.

### Mark 1:35-39

[35] And in the morning, rising up a great while before day, he went out, and departed into a solitary place, and there prayed.
[36] And Simon and they that were with him followed after him.
[37] And when they had found him, they said unto him, All men seek for thee.
[38] And he said unto them, Let us go into the next towns, that I may preach there also: for therefore came I forth.
[39] And he preached in their synagogues throughout all Galilee, and cast out devils.

### Luke 4:42-44

[42] And when it was day, he departed and went into a desert place: and the people sought him, and came unto him, and stayed him, that he should not depart from them.
[43] And he said unto them, I must preach the kingdom of God to other cities also: for therefore am I sent.
[44] And he preached in the synagogues of Galilee.

## 2. Jesus Cures Man With Leprosy

### Matthew 8:1-4; Mark 1:40-45; Luke 5:12-16

#### Matthew 8:1-4

[1] When he was come down from the mountain, great multitudes followed him.
[2] And, behold, there came a leper and worshipped him, saying, Lord, if thou wilt, thou canst make me clean.
[3] And Jesus put forth his hand, and touched him, saying, I will; be thou clean. And immediately his leprosy was cleansed.
[4] And Jesus saith unto him, See thou tell no man; but go thy way, shew thyself to the priest, and offer the gift that Moses commanded, for a testimony unto them.

Healing Examples From The New Testament: The Gospels

## Mark 1:40-45

40 And there came a leper to him, beseeching him, and kneeling down to him, and saying unto him, If thou wilt, thou canst make me clean.

41 And Jesus, moved with compassion, put forth his hand, and touched him, and saith unto him, I will; be thou clean.

42 And as soon as he had spoken, immediately the leprosy departed from him, and he was cleansed.

43 And he straitly charged him, and forthwith sent him away;

44 And saith unto him, See thou say nothing to any man: but go thy way, shew thyself to the priest, and offer for thy cleansing those things which Moses commanded, for a testimony unto them.

45 But he went out, and began to publish it much, and to blaze abroad the matter, insomuch that Jesus could no more openly enter into the city, but was without in desert places: and they came to him from every quarter.

## Luke 5:12-16

12 And it came to pass, when he was in a certain city, behold a man full of leprosy: who seeing Jesus fell on his face, and besought him, saying, Lord, if thou wilt, thou canst make me clean.

13 And he put forth his hand, and touched him, saying, I will: be thou clean. And immediately the leprosy departed from him.

14 And he charged him to tell no man: but go, and shew thyself to the priest, and offer for thy cleansing, according as Moses commanded, for a testimony unto them.

15 But so much the more went there a fame abroad of him: and great multitudes came together to hear, and to be healed by him of their infirmities.

16 And he withdrew himself into the wilderness, and prayed.

Healing Examples From The New Testament: The Gospels

## 3.  Jesus Heals the Roman Centurion's Servant

### Matthew 8:5-13; Luke 7:1-10

### Matthew 8:5-13

5 And when Jesus was entered into Capernaum, there came unto him a centurion, beseeching him,
6 And saying, Lord, my servant lieth at home sick of the palsy, grievously tormented.
7 And Jesus saith unto him, I will come and heal him.
8 The centurion answered and said, Lord, I am not worthy that thou shouldest come under my roof: but speak the word only, and my servant shall be healed.
9 For I am a man under authority, having soldiers under me: and I say to this man, Go, and he goeth; and to another, Come, and he cometh; and to my servant, Do this, and he doeth it.
10 When Jesus heard it, he marvelled, and said to them that followed, Verily I say unto you, I have not found so great faith, no, not in Israel.
11 And I say unto you, That many shall come from the east and west, and shall sit down with Abraham, and Isaac, and Jacob, in the kingdom of heaven.
12 But the children of the kingdom shall be cast out into outer darkness: there shall be weeping and gnashing of teeth.
13 And Jesus said unto the centurion, Go thy way; and as thou hast believed, so be it done unto thee. And his servant was healed in the selfsame hour.

### Luke 7:1-10

1 Now when he had ended all his sayings in the audience of the people, he entered into Capernaum.
2 And a certain centurion's servant, who was dear unto him, was sick, and ready to die.

Healing Examples From The New Testament: The Gospels

³ And when he heard of Jesus, he sent unto him the elders of the Jews, beseeching him that he would come and heal his servant.
⁴ And when they came to Jesus, they besought him instantly, saying, That he was worthy for whom he should do this:
⁵ For he loveth our nation, and he hath built us a synagogue.
⁶ Then Jesus went with them. And when he was now not far from the house, the centurion sent friends to him, saying unto him, Lord, trouble not thyself: for I am not worthy that thou shouldest enter under my roof:
⁷ Wherefore neither thought I myself worthy to come unto thee: but say in a word, and my servant shall be healed.
⁸ For I also am a man set under authority, having under me soldiers, and I say unto one, Go, and he goeth; and to another, Come, and he cometh; and to my servant, Do this, and he doeth it.
⁹ When Jesus heard these things, he marvelled at him, and turned him about, and said unto the people that followed him, I say unto you, I have not found so great faith, no, not in Israel.
¹⁰ And they that were sent, returning to the house, found the servant whole that had been sick.

## 4. Jesus Heals Peter's Mother-In-Law

### Matthew 8:14-15; Mark 1:29-31; Luke 4:38-39

#### Matthew 8:14-15

¹⁴ And when Jesus was come into Peter's house, he saw his wife's mother laid, and sick of a fever.
¹⁵ And he touched her hand, and the fever left her: and she arose, and ministered unto them.

## Mark 1:29-31

⁹ And forthwith, when they were come out of the synagogue, they entered into the house of Simon and Andrew, with James and John.
³⁰ But Simon's wife's mother lay sick of a fever, and anon they tell him of her.
³¹ And he came and took her by the hand, and lifted her up; and immediately the fever left her, and she ministered unto them.

## Luke 4:38-39

³⁸ And he arose out of the synagogue, and entered into Simon's house. And Simon's wife's mother was taken with a great fever; and they besought him for her.
³⁹ And he stood over her, and rebuked the fever; and it left her: and immediately she arose and ministered unto them.

# 5. Jesus Heals Many Sick in the Evening at Peter's House in Capernaum

## Matthew 8:16-17; Mark 1:32-34; Luke 4:40-41

### Matthew 8:16-17

¹⁶ When the even was come, they brought unto him many that were possessed with devils: and he cast out the spirits with his word, and healed all that were sick:
¹⁷ That it might be fulfilled which was spoken by Esaias the prophet, saying, Himself took our infirmities, and bare our sicknesses.

### Mark 1:32-34

³² And at even, when the sun did set, they brought unto him all that were diseased, and them that were possessed with devils.
³³ And all the city was gathered together at the door.

34 And he healed many that were sick of divers diseases, and cast out many devils; and suffered not the devils to speak, because they knew him.

### Luke 4:40-41

40 Now when the sun was setting, all they that had any sick with divers diseases brought them unto him; and he laid his hands on every one of them, and healed them.
41 And devils also came out of many, crying out, and saying, Thou art Christ the Son of God. And he rebuking them suffered them not to speak: for they knew that he was Christ.

## 6.  Jesus Casts Demons Into Herd of Pigs

### Matthew 8:28-34; Mark 5:1-20; Luke 8:26-39

### Matthew 8:28-34

28 And when he was come to the other side into the country of the Gergesenes, there met him two possessed with devils, coming out of the tombs, exceeding fierce, so that no man might pass by that way.
29 And, behold, they cried out, saying, What have we to do with thee, Jesus, thou Son of God? art thou come hither to torment us before the time?
30 And there was a good way off from them an herd of many swine feeding.
31 So the devils besought him, saying, If thou cast us out, suffer us to go away into the herd of swine.
32 And he said unto them, Go. And when they were come out, they went into the herd of swine: and, behold, the whole herd of swine ran violently down a steep place into the sea, and perished in the waters.
33 And they that kept them fled, and went their ways into the city, and told every thing, and what was befallen to the possessed of the devils.

³⁴ And, behold, the whole city came out to meet Jesus: and when they saw him, they besought him that he would depart out of their coasts.

## Mark 5:1-20

¹ And they came over unto the other side of the sea, into the country of the Gadarenes.
² And when he was come out of the ship, immediately there met him out of the tombs a man with an unclean spirit,
³ Who had his dwelling among the tombs; and no man could bind him, no, not with chains:
⁴ Because that he had been often bound with fetters and chains, and the chains had been plucked asunder by him, and the fetters broken in pieces: neither could any man tame him.
⁵ And always, night and day, he was in the mountains, and in the tombs, crying, and cutting himself with stones.
⁶ But when he saw Jesus afar off, he ran and worshipped him,
⁷ And cried with a loud voice, and said, What have I to do with thee, Jesus, thou Son of the most high God? I adjure thee by God, that thou torment me not.
⁸ For he said unto him, Come out of the man, thou unclean spirit.
⁹ And he asked him, What is thy name? And he answered, saying, My name is Legion: for we are many.
¹⁰ And he besought him much that he would not send them away out of the country.
¹¹ Now there was there nigh unto the mountains a great herd of swine feeding.
¹² And all the devils besought him, saying, Send us into the swine, that we may enter into them.
¹³ And forthwith Jesus gave them leave. And the unclean spirits went out, and entered into the swine: and the herd ran violently down a steep place into the sea, (they were about two thousand;) and were choked in the sea.

## Healing Examples From The New Testament: The Gospels

¹⁴ And they that fed the swine fled, and told it in the city, and in the country. And they went out to see what it was that was done.

¹⁵ And they come to Jesus, and see him that was possessed with the devil, and had the legion, sitting, and clothed, and in his right mind: and they were afraid.

¹⁶ And they that saw it told them how it befell to him that was possessed with the devil, and also concerning the swine.

¹⁷ And they began to pray him to depart out of their coasts.

¹⁸ And when he was come into the ship, he that had been possessed with the devil prayed him that he might be with him.

¹⁹ Howbeit Jesus suffered him not, but saith unto him, Go home to thy friends, and tell them how great things the Lord hath done for thee, and hath had compassion on thee.

²⁰ And he departed, and began to publish in Decapolis how great things Jesus had done for him: and all men did marvel.

## Luke 8:26-39

²⁶ And they arrived at the country of the Gadarenes, which is over against Galilee.

²⁷ And when he went forth to land, there met him out of the city a certain man, which had devils long time, and ware no clothes, neither abode in any house, but in the tombs.

²⁸ When he saw Jesus, he cried out, and fell down before him, and with a loud voice said, What have I to do with thee, Jesus, thou Son of God most high? I beseech thee, torment me not.

²⁹ (For he had commanded the unclean spirit to come out of the man. For oftentimes it had caught him: and he was kept bound with chains and in fetters; and he brake the bands, and was driven of the devil into the wilderness.)

³⁰ And Jesus asked him, saying, What is thy name? And he said, Legion: because many devils were entered into him.

³¹ And they besought him that he would not command them to go out into the deep.

32 And there was there an herd of many swine feeding on the mountain: and they besought him that he would suffer them to enter into them. And he suffered them.
33 Then went the devils out of the man, and entered into the swine: and the herd ran violently down a steep place into the lake, and were choked.
34 When they that fed them saw what was done, they fled, and went and told it in the city and in the country.
35 Then they went out to see what was done; and came to Jesus, and found the man, out of whom the devils were departed, sitting at the feet of Jesus, clothed, and in his right mind: and they were afraid.
36 They also which saw it told them by what means he that was possessed of the devils was healed.
37 Then the whole multitude of the country of the Gadarenes round about besought him to depart from them; for they were taken with great fear: and he went up into the ship, and returned back again.
38 Now the man out of whom the devils were departed besought him that he might be with him: but Jesus sent him away, saying,
39 Return to thine own house, and shew how great things God hath done unto thee. And he went his way, and published throughout the whole city how great things Jesus had done unto him.

## 7. Jesus Forgives and Heals Paralytic Lowered Through the Roof

### Matthew 9:1-8; Mark 2:1-12; Luke 5:17-26

#### Matthew 9:1-8

1 And he entered into a ship, and passed over, and came into his own city.
2 And, behold, they brought to him a man sick of the palsy, lying on a bed: and Jesus seeing their faith said unto the

sick of the palsy; Son, be of good cheer; thy sins be forgiven thee.
3 And, behold, certain of the scribes said within themselves, This man blasphemeth.
4 And Jesus knowing their thoughts said, Wherefore think ye evil in your hearts?
5 For whether is easier, to say, Thy sins be forgiven thee; or to say, Arise, and walk?
6 But that ye may know that the Son of man hath power on earth to forgive sins, (then saith he to the sick of the palsy,) Arise, take up thy bed, and go unto thine house.
7 And he arose, and departed to his house.
8 But when the multitudes saw it, they marvelled, and glorified God, which had given such power unto men.

## Mark 2:1-12

1 And again he entered into Capernaum after some days; and it was noised that he was in the house.
2 And straightway many were gathered together, insomuch that there was no room to receive them, no, not so much as about the door: and he preached the word unto them.
3 And they come unto him, bringing one sick of the palsy, which was borne of four.
4 And when they could not come nigh unto him for the press, they uncovered the roof where he was: and when they had broken it up, they let down the bed wherein the sick of the palsy lay.
5 When Jesus saw their faith, he said unto the sick of the palsy, Son, thy sins be forgiven thee.
6 But there was certain of the scribes sitting there, and reasoning in their hearts,
7 Why doth this man thus speak blasphemies? who can forgive sins but God only?
8 And immediately when Jesus perceived in his spirit that they so reasoned within themselves, he said unto them, Why reason ye these things in your hearts?

9 Whether is it easier to say to the sick of the palsy, Thy sins be forgiven thee; or to say, Arise, and take up thy bed, and walk?

10 But that ye may know that the Son of man hath power on earth to forgive sins, (he saith to the sick of the palsy,)

11 I say unto thee, Arise, and take up thy bed, and go thy way into thine house.

12 And immediately he arose, took up the bed, and went forth before them all; insomuch that they were all amazed, and glorified God, saying, We never saw it on this fashion.

## Luke 5:17-26

17 And it came to pass on a certain day, as he was teaching, that there were Pharisees and doctors of the law sitting by, which were come out of every town of Galilee, and Judaea, and Jerusalem: and the power of the Lord was present to heal them.

18 And, behold, men brought in a bed a man which was taken with a palsy: and they sought means to bring him in, and to lay him before him.

19 And when they could not find by what way they might bring him in because of the multitude, they went upon the housetop, and let him down through the tiling with his couch into the midst before Jesus.

20 And when he saw their faith, he said unto him, Man, thy sins are forgiven thee.

21 And the scribes and the Pharisees began to reason, saying, Who is this which speaketh blasphemies? Who can forgive sins, but God alone?

22 But when Jesus perceived their thoughts, he answering said unto them, What reason ye in your hearts?

23 Whether is easier, to say, Thy sins be forgiven thee; or to say, Rise up and walk?

24 But that ye may know that the Son of man hath power upon earth to forgive sins, (he said unto the sick of the palsy,) I say unto thee, Arise, and take up thy couch, and go into thine house.

25 And immediately he rose up before them, and took up that whereon he lay, and departed to his own house, glorifying God.
26 And they were all amazed, and they glorified God, and were filled with fear, saying, We have seen strange things to day.

## 8. Jesus Raises Jarius' Daughter (Synagogue Leader)

### Matthew 9:18-19, 9:23-26; Mark 5:21-24; Luke 8:40-42; 8:49-56

**Matthew 9:18-19, 23-26**

18 While he spake these things unto them, behold, there came a certain ruler, and worshipped him, saying, My daughter is even now dead: but come and lay thy hand upon her, and she shall live.
19 And Jesus arose, and followed him, and so did his disciples.

23 And when Jesus came into the ruler's house, and saw the minstrels and the people making a noise,
24 He said unto them, Give place: for the maid is not dead, but sleepeth. And they laughed him to scorn.
25 But when the people were put forth, he went in, and took her by the hand, and the maid arose.
26 And the fame hereof went abroad into all that land.

**Mark 5:21-24**

21 And when Jesus was passed over again by ship unto the other side, much people gathered unto him: and he was nigh unto the sea.
22 And, behold, there cometh one of the rulers of the synagogue, Jairus by name; and when he saw him, he fell at his feet,

23 And besought him greatly, saying, My little daughter lieth at the point of death: I pray thee, come and lay thy hands on her, that she may be healed; and she shall live.
24 And Jesus went with him; and much people followed him, and thronged him.

Mark 5:35-43

35 While he yet spake, there came from the ruler of the synagogue's house certain which said, Thy daughter is dead: why troublest thou the Master any further?
36 As soon as Jesus heard the word that was spoken, he saith unto the ruler of the synagogue, Be not afraid, only believe.
37 And he suffered no man to follow him, save Peter, and James, and John the brother of James.
38 And he cometh to the house of the ruler of the synagogue, and seeth the tumult, and them that wept and wailed greatly.
39 And when he was come in, he saith unto them, Why make ye this ado, and weep? the damsel is not dead, but sleepeth.
40 And they laughed him to scorn. But when he had put them all out, he taketh the father and the mother of the damsel, and them that were with him, and entereth in where the damsel was lying.
41 And he took the damsel by the hand, and said unto her, Talitha cumi; which is, being interpreted, Damsel, I say unto thee, arise.
42 And straightway the damsel arose, and walked; for she was of the age of twelve years. And they were astonished with a great astonishment.
43 And he charged them straitly that no man should know it; and commanded that something should be given her to eat.

## Luke 8:40-42, 49-56

40 And it came to pass, that, when Jesus was returned, the people gladly received him: for they were all waiting for him.

## Healing Examples From The New Testament: The Gospels

⁴¹ And, behold, there came a man named Jairus, and he was a ruler of the synagogue: and he fell down at Jesus' feet, and besought him that he would come into his house:

⁴² For he had one only daughter, about twelve years of age, and she lay a dying. But as he went the people thronged him.

⁴⁹ While he yet spake, there cometh one from the ruler of the synagogue's house, saying to him, Thy daughter is dead; trouble not the Master.

⁵⁰ But when Jesus heard it, he answered him, saying, Fear not: believe only, and she shall be made whole.

⁵¹ And when he came into the house, he suffered no man to go in, save Peter, and James, and John, and the father and the mother of the maiden.

⁵² And all wept, and bewailed her: but he said, Weep not; she is not dead, but sleepeth.

⁵³ And they laughed him to scorn, knowing that she was dead.

⁵⁴ And he put them all out, and took her by the hand, and called, saying, Maid, arise.

⁵⁵ And her spirit came again, and she arose straightway: and he commanded to give her meat.

⁵⁶ And her parents were astonished: but he charged them that they should tell no man what was done.

## 9. Jesus Cures Woman With the Issue of Blood

### Matthew 9:20-22; Mark 5:25-34; Luke 8:42-48

### Matthew 9:20-22

²⁰ And, behold, a woman, which was diseased with an issue of blood twelve years, came behind him, and touched the hem of his garment:

21 For she said within herself, If I may but touch his garment, I shall be whole.
22 But Jesus turned him about, and when he saw her, he said, Daughter, be of good comfort; thy faith hath made thee whole. And the woman was made whole from that hour.

## Mark 5:25-34

25 And a certain woman, which had an issue of blood twelve years,
26 And had suffered many things of many physicians, and had spent all that she had, and was nothing bettered, but rather grew worse,
27 When she had heard of Jesus, came in the press behind, and touched his garment.
28 For she said, If I may touch but his clothes, I shall be whole.
29 And straightway the fountain of her blood was dried up; and she felt in her body that she was healed of that plague.
30 And Jesus, immediately knowing in himself that virtue had gone out of him, turned him about in the press, and said, Who touched my clothes?
31 And his disciples said unto him, Thou seest the multitude thronging thee, and sayest thou, Who touched me?
32 And he looked round about to see her that had done this thing.
33 But the woman fearing and trembling, knowing what was done in her, came and fell down before him, and told him all the truth.
34 And he said unto her, Daughter, thy faith hath made thee whole; go in peace, and be whole of thy plague.

## Luke 8:42b-48

42 For he had one only daughter, about twelve years of age, and she lay a dying. But as he went the people thronged him.

43 And a woman having an issue of blood twelve years, which had spent all her living upon physicians, neither could be healed of any,
44 Came behind him, and touched the border of his garment: and immediately her issue of blood stanched.
45 And Jesus said, Who touched me? When all denied, Peter and they that were with him said, Master, the multitude throng thee and press thee, and sayest thou, Who touched me?
46 And Jesus said, Somebody hath touched me: for I perceive that virtue is gone out of me.
47 And when the woman saw that she was not hid, she came trembling, and falling down before him, she declared unto him before all the people for what cause she had touched him, and how she was healed immediately.
48 And he said unto her, Daughter, be of good comfort: thy faith hath made thee whole; go in peace.

## 10. Jesus Gives Sight to Two Blind Men

### Matthew 9:27-31

27 And when Jesus departed thence, two blind men followed him, crying, and saying, Thou son of David, have mercy on us.
28 And when he was come into the house, the blind men came to him: and Jesus saith unto them, Believe ye that I am able to do this? They said unto him, Yea, Lord.
29 Then touched he their eyes, saying, According to your faith be it unto you.
30 And their eyes were opened; and Jesus straitly charged them, saying, See that no man know it.
31 But they, when they were departed, spread abroad his fame in all that country.

Healing Examples From The New Testament: The Gospels

## 11. Jesus Heals Mute Demonic

### Matthew 9:32-33

32 As they went out, behold, they brought to him a dumb man possessed with a devil.
33 And when the devil was cast out, the dumb spake: and the multitudes marvelled, saying, It was never so seen in Israel.

## 12. Jesus Teaching, Preaching and Healing Every Sickness and Disease

### Matthew 9:35

35 And Jesus went about all the cities and villages, teaching in their synagogues, and preaching the gospel of the kingdom, and healing every sickness and every disease among the people.

## 13. Jesus Sends the Twelve Disciples to Preach and Heal

### Matthew 10:1-8; Mark 6:6-13; Luke 9:1-6

### Matthew 10:1-8

1 And when he had called unto him his twelve disciples, he gave them power against unclean spirits, to cast them out, and to heal all manner of sickness and all manner of disease.
2 Now the names of the twelve apostles are these; The first, Simon, who is called Peter, and Andrew his brother; James the son of Zebedee, and John his brother;
3 Philip, and Bartholomew; Thomas, and Matthew the publican; James the son of Alphaeus, and Lebbaeus, whose surname was Thaddaeus;
4 Simon the Canaanite, and Judas Iscariot, who also betrayed him.

5 These twelve Jesus sent forth, and commanded them, saying, Go not into the way of the Gentiles, and into any city of the Samaritans enter ye not:
6 But go rather to the lost sheep of the house of Israel.
7 And as ye go, preach, saying, The kingdom of heaven is at hand.
8 Heal the sick, cleanse the lepers, raise the dead, cast out devils: freely ye have received, freely give.

## Mark 6:6-13

6 And he marvelled because of their unbelief. And he went round about the villages, teaching.
7 And he called unto him the twelve, and began to send them forth by two and two; and gave them power over unclean spirits;
8 And commanded them that they should take nothing for their journey, save a staff only; no scrip, no bread, no money in their purse:
9 But be shod with sandals; and not put on two coats.
10 And he said unto them, In what place soever ye enter into an house, there abide till ye depart from that place.
11 And whosoever shall not receive you, nor hear you, when ye depart thence, shake off the dust under your feet for a testimony against them. Verily I say unto you, It shall be more tolerable for Sodom and Gomorrha in the day of judgment, than for that city.
12 And they went out, and preached that men should repent.
13 And they cast out many devils, and anointed with oil many that were sick, and healed them.

## Luke 9:1-9

1 Then he called his twelve disciples together, and gave them power and authority over all devils, and to cure diseases.
2 And he sent them to preach the kingdom of God, and to heal the sick.

3 And he said unto them, Take nothing for your journey, neither staves, nor scrip, neither bread, neither money; neither have two coats apiece.
4 And whatsoever house ye enter into, there abide, and thence depart.
5 And whosoever will not receive you, when ye go out of that city, shake off the very dust from your feet for a testimony against them.
6 And they departed, and went through the towns, preaching the gospel, and healing every where.
7 Now Herod the tetrarch heard of all that was done by him: and he was perplexed, because that it was said of some, that John was risen from the dead;
8 And of some, that Elias had appeared; and of others, that one of the old prophets was risen again.
9 And Herod said, John have I beheaded: but who is this, of whom I hear such things? And he desired to see him.

## 14. Jesus Healed Many – Answers John the Baptist's Disciples

### Matthew 11:2-5; Luke 7:20-23

### Matthew 11:2-5

2 Now when John had heard in the prison the works of Christ, he sent two of his disciples,
3 And said unto him, Art thou he that should come, or do we look for another?
4 Jesus answered and said unto them, Go and shew John again those things which ye do hear and see:
5 The blind receive their sight, and the lame walk, the lepers are cleansed, and the deaf hear, the dead are raised up, and the poor have the gospel preached to them.

### Luke 7:20-23

20 John's two disciples found Jesus and said to him, "John the Baptist sent us to ask, 'Are you the Messiah we've been expecting, or should we keep looking for someone else?'"
21 At that very time, Jesus cured many people of their diseases, illnesses, and evil spirits, and he restored sight to many who were blind. 22 Then he told John's disciples, "Go back to John and tell him what you have seen and heard—the blind see, the lame walk, the lepers are cured, the deaf hear, the dead are raised to life, and the Good News is being preached to the poor. 23 And tell him, 'God blesses those who do not turn away because of me.[c]'

## 15. Jesus Heals Man with a Withered Hand

### Matthew 12:9-14; Mark 3:1-6; Luke 6:6-11

### Matthew 12:9-14

9 And when he was departed thence, he went into their synagogue:
10 And, behold, there was a man which had his hand withered. And they asked him, saying, Is it lawful to heal on the sabbath days? that they might accuse him.
11 And he said unto them, What man shall there be among you, that shall have one sheep, and if it fall into a pit on the sabbath day, will he not lay hold on it, and lift it out?
12 How much then is a man better than a sheep? Wherefore it is lawful to do well on the sabbath days.
13 Then saith he to the man, Stretch forth thine hand. And he stretched it forth; and it was restored whole, like as the other.
14 Then the Pharisees went out, and held a council against him, how they might destroy him.

Healing Examples From The New Testament: The Gospels

## Mark 3:1-6

¹ And he entered again into the synagogue; and there was a man there which had a withered hand.

² And they watched him, whether he would heal him on the sabbath day; that they might accuse him.

³ And he saith unto the man which had the withered hand, Stand forth.

⁴ And he saith unto them, Is it lawful to do good on the sabbath days, or to do evil? to save life, or to kill? But they held their peace.

⁵ And when he had looked round about on them with anger, being grieved for the hardness of their hearts, he saith unto the man, Stretch forth thine hand. And he stretched it out: and his hand was restored whole as the other.

⁶ And the Pharisees went forth, and straightway took counsel with the Herodians against him, how they might destroy him.

## Luke 6:6-11

⁶ And it came to pass also on another sabbath, that he entered into the synagogue and taught: and there was a man whose right hand was withered.

⁷ And the scribes and Pharisees watched him, whether he would heal on the sabbath day; that they might find an accusation against him.

⁸ But he knew their thoughts, and said to the man which had the withered hand, Rise up, and stand forth in the midst. And he arose and stood forth.

⁹ Then said Jesus unto them, I will ask you one thing; Is it lawful on the sabbath days to do good, or to do evil? to save life, or to destroy it?

¹⁰ And looking round about upon them all, he said unto the man, Stretch forth thy hand. And he did so: and his hand was restored whole as the other.

¹¹ And they were filled with madness; and communed one with another what they might do to Jesus.

Healing Examples From The New Testament: The Gospels

## 16. Jesus Heals Many By the Sea

### Matthew 12:15-21; Mark 3:7-12; Luke 6:17-19
### Matthew 12:15-21

15 But when Jesus knew it, he withdrew himself from thence: and great multitudes followed him, and he healed them all;
16 And charged them that they should not make him known:
17 That it might be fulfilled which was spoken by Esaias the prophet, saying,
18 Behold my servant, whom I have chosen; my beloved, in whom my soul is well pleased: I will put my spirit upon him, and he shall shew judgment to the Gentiles.
19 He shall not strive, nor cry; neither shall any man hear his voice in the streets.
20 A bruised reed shall he not break, and smoking flax shall he not quench, till he send forth judgment unto victory.
21 And in his name shall the Gentiles trust.

### Mark 3:7-12

7 But Jesus withdrew himself with his disciples to the sea: and a great multitude from Galilee followed him, and from Judaea,
8 And from Jerusalem, and from Idumaea, and from beyond Jordan; and they about Tyre and Sidon, a great multitude, when they had heard what great things he did, came unto him.
9 And he spake to his disciples, that a small ship should wait on him because of the multitude, lest they should throng him.
10 For he had healed many; insomuch that they pressed upon him for to touch him, as many as had plagues.
11 And unclean spirits, when they saw him, fell down before him, and cried, saying, Thou art the Son of God.

## Luke 6:17-19

17 And he came down with them, and stood in the plain, and the company of his disciples, and a great multitude of people out of all Judaea and Jerusalem, and from the sea coast of Tyre and Sidon, which came to hear him, and to be healed of their diseases;
18 And they that were vexed with unclean spirits: and they were healed.
19 And the whole multitude sought to touch him: for there went virtue out of him, and healed them all.

## 17. Jesus Heals the Blind and Mute Demoniac

### Matthew 12:22-28; Luke 11:14-26

#### Matthew 12:22-28

22 Then was brought unto him one possessed with a devil, blind, and dumb: and he healed him, insomuch that the blind and dumb both spake and saw.
23 And all the people were amazed, and said, Is not this the son of David?
24 But when the Pharisees heard it, they said, This fellow doth not cast out devils, but by Beelzebub the prince of the devils.
25 And Jesus knew their thoughts, and said unto them, Every kingdom divided against itself is brought to desolation; and every city or house divided against itself shall not stand:
26 And if Satan cast out Satan, he is divided against himself; how shall then his kingdom stand?
27 And if I by Beelzebub cast out devils, by whom do your children cast them out? therefore they shall be your judges.
28 But if I cast out devils by the Spirit of God, then the kingdom of God is come unto you.

## Luke 11:14-26

¹⁴ And he was casting out a devil, and it was dumb. And it came to pass, when the devil was gone out, the dumb spake; and the people wondered.

¹⁵ But some of them said, He casteth out devils through Beelzebub the chief of the devils.

¹⁶ And others, tempting him, sought of him a sign from heaven.

¹⁷ But he, knowing their thoughts, said unto them, Every kingdom divided against itself is brought to desolation; and a house divided against a house falleth.

¹⁸ If Satan also be divided against himself, how shall his kingdom stand? because ye say that I cast out devils through Beelzebub.

¹⁹ And if I by Beelzebub cast out devils, by whom do your sons cast them out? therefore shall they be your judges.

²⁰ But if I with the finger of God cast out devils, no doubt the kingdom of God is come upon you.

²¹ When a strong man armed keepeth his palace, his goods are in peace:

²² But when a stronger than he shall come upon him, and overcome him, he taketh from him all his armour wherein he trusted, and divideth his spoils.

²³ He that is not with me is against me: and he that gathereth not with me scattereth.

²⁴ When the unclean spirit is gone out of a man, he walketh through dry places, seeking rest; and finding none, he saith, I will return unto my house whence I came out.

²⁵ And when he cometh, he findeth it swept and garnished.

²⁶ Then goeth he, and taketh to him seven other spirits more wicked than himself; and they enter in, and dwell there: and the last state of that man is worse than the first.

Healing Examples From The New Testament: The Gospels

## 18. Jesus Did Few Miracles Because of Their Lack of Faith

### Matthew 13:58; Mark 6:4-6

### Matthew 13:58

58 And he did not many mighty works there because of their unbelief.

### Mark 6:4-6

4 But Jesus, said unto them, A prophet is not without honour, but in his own country, and among his own kin, and in his own house.
5 And he could there do no mighty work, save that he laid his hands upon a few sick folk, and healed them.
6 And he marvelled because of their unbelief. And he went round about the villages, teaching.

## 19. Jesus Heals Their Sick (Before Feeding the 5,000)

### Matthew 14:14; Luke 9:11; John 6:1

### Matthew 14:14

14 And Jesus went forth, and saw a great multitude, and was moved with compassion toward them, and he healed their sick.

### Luke 9:11

11 And the people, when they knew it, followed him: and he received them, and spake unto them of the kingdom of God, and healed them that had need of healing.

**John 6:1**

¹ After these things Jesus went over the sea of Galilee, which is the sea of Tiberias.

## 20. Jesus Heals Many at Gennesaret

### Matthew 14:34-36; Mark 6:53-56
### Matthew 14:34-36

³⁴ And when they were gone over, they came into the land of Gennesaret.
³⁵ And when the men of that place had knowledge of him, they sent out into all that country round about, and brought unto him all that were diseased;
³⁶ And besought him that they might only touch the hem of his garment: and as many as touched were made perfectly whole.

### Mark 6:53-56

⁵³ And when they had passed over, they came into the land of Gennesaret, and drew to the shore.
⁵⁴ And when they were come out of the ship, straightway they knew him,
⁵⁵ And ran through that whole region round about, and began to carry about in beds those that were sick, where they heard he was.
⁵⁶ And whithersoever he entered, into villages, or cities, or country, they laid the sick in the streets, and besought him that they might touch if it were but the border of his garment: and as many as touched him were made whole.

## 21. Jesus Heals the Canaanite Woman's Demon-Possessed Daughter

### Matthew 15:21-28; Mark 7:24-30

### Matthew 15:21-28

21 Then Jesus went thence, and departed into the coasts of Tyre and Sidon.
22 And, behold, a woman of Canaan came out of the same coasts, and cried unto him, saying, Have mercy on me, O Lord, thou son of David; my daughter is grievously vexed with a devil.
23 But he answered her not a word. And his disciples came and besought him, saying, Send her away; for she crieth after us.
24 But he answered and said, I am not sent but unto the lost sheep of the house of Israel.
25 Then came she and worshipped him, saying, Lord, help me.
26 But he answered and said, It is not meet to take the children's bread, and to cast it to dogs.
27 And she said, Truth, Lord: yet the dogs eat of the crumbs which fall from their masters' table.
28 Then Jesus answered and said unto her, O woman, great is thy faith: be it unto thee even as thou wilt. And her daughter was made whole from that very hour.

### Mark 7:24-30

24 And from thence he arose, and went into the borders of Tyre and Sidon, and entered into an house, and would have no man know it: but he could not be hid.
25 For a certain woman, whose young daughter had an unclean spirit, heard of him, and came and fell at his feet:
26 The woman was a Greek, a Syrophenician by nation; and she besought him that he would cast forth the devil out of her daughter.

27 But Jesus said unto her, Let the children first be filled: for it is not meet to take the children's bread, and to cast it unto the dogs.
28 And she answered and said unto him, Yes, Lord: yet the dogs under the table eat of the children's crumbs.
29 And he said unto her, For this saying go thy way; the devil is gone out of thy daughter.
30 And when she was come to her house, she found the devil gone out, and her daughter laid upon the bed.

## 22. Lame, Blind, Maimed, Mute Laid at Jesus Feet

### Matthew 15:29-30

29 And Jesus departed from thence, and came nigh unto the sea of Galilee; and went up into a mountain, and sat down there.
30 And great multitudes came unto him, having with them those that were lame, blind, dumb, maimed, and many others, and cast them down at Jesus' feet; and he healed them:

## 23. Jesus Heals the Boy With a Demon (Seizures)

### Matthew 17:14-21; Mark 9:14-29; Luke 9:37-43
### Matthew 17:14-21

14 And when they were come to the multitude, there came to him a certain man, kneeling down to him, and saying,
15 Lord, have mercy on my son: for he is lunatick, and sore vexed: for ofttimes he falleth into the fire, and oft into the water.
16 And I brought him to thy disciples, and they could not cure him.
17 Then Jesus answered and said, O faithless and perverse generation, how long shall I be with you? how long shall I suffer you? bring him hither to me.

## Healing Examples From The New Testament: The Gospels

18 And Jesus rebuked the devil; and he departed out of him: and the child was cured from that very hour.
19 Then came the disciples to Jesus apart, and said, Why could not we cast him out?
20 And Jesus said unto them, Because of your unbelief: for verily I say unto you, If ye have faith as a grain of mustard seed, ye shall say unto this mountain, Remove hence to yonder place; and it shall remove; and nothing shall be impossible unto you.
21 Howbeit this kind goeth not out but by prayer and fasting.

## Mark 9:14-29

14 And when he came to his disciples, he saw a great multitude about them, and the scribes questioning with them.
15 And straightway all the people, when they beheld him, were greatly amazed, and running to him saluted him.
16 And he asked the scribes, What question ye with them?
17 And one of the multitude answered and said, Master, I have brought unto thee my son, which hath a dumb spirit;
18 And wheresoever he taketh him, he teareth him: and he foameth, and gnasheth with his teeth, and pineth away: and I spake to thy disciples that they should cast him out; and they could not.
19 He answereth him, and saith, O faithless generation, how long shall I be with you? how long shall I suffer you? bring him unto me.
20 And they brought him unto him: and when he saw him, straightway the spirit tare him; and he fell on the ground, and wallowed foaming.
21 And he asked his father, How long is it ago since this came unto him? And he said, Of a child.
22 And ofttimes it hath cast him into the fire, and into the waters, to destroy him: but if thou canst do any thing, have compassion on us, and help us.
23 Jesus said unto him, If thou canst believe, all things are possible to him that believeth.

24 And straightway the father of the child cried out, and said with tears, Lord, I believe; help thou mine unbelief.
25 When Jesus saw that the people came running together, he rebuked the foul spirit, saying unto him, Thou dumb and deaf spirit, I charge thee, come out of him, and enter no more into him.
26 And the spirit cried, and rent him sore, and came out of him: and he was as one dead; insomuch that many said, He is dead.
27 But Jesus took him by the hand, and lifted him up; and he arose.
28 And when he was come into the house, his disciples asked him privately, Why could not we cast him out?
29 And he said unto them, This kind can come forth by nothing, but by prayer and fasting.

## Luke 9:37-43a

37 And it came to pass, that on the next day, when they were come down from the hill, much people met him.
38 And, behold, a man of the company cried out, saying, Master, I beseech thee, look upon my son: for he is mine only child.
39 And, lo, a spirit taketh him, and he suddenly crieth out; and it teareth him that he foameth again, and bruising him hardly departeth from him.
40 And I besought thy disciples to cast him out; and they could not.
41 And Jesus answering said, O faithless and perverse generation, how long shall I be with you, and suffer you? Bring thy son hither.
42 And as he was yet a coming, the devil threw him down, and tare him. And Jesus rebuked the unclean spirit, and healed the child, and delivered him again to his father.
43 And they were all amazed at the mighty power of God. But while they wondered every one at all things which Jesus did, he said unto his disciples,

Healing Examples From The New Testament: The Gospels

# 24. Jesus Restores of Sight to Blind Bartimaeus on the Side of the Road

## Matthew 20:29-34; Mark 10:46-52; Luke 18:35-43

### Matthew 20:29-34

29 And as they departed from Jericho, a great multitude followed him.
30 And, behold, two blind men sitting by the way side, when they heard that Jesus passed by, cried out, saying, Have mercy on us, O Lord, thou son of David.
31 And the multitude rebuked them, because they should hold their peace: but they cried the more, saying, Have mercy on us, O Lord, thou son of David.
32 And Jesus stood still, and called them, and said, What will ye that I shall do unto you?
33 They say unto him, Lord, that our eyes may be opened.
34 So Jesus had compassion on them, and touched their eyes: and immediately their eyes received sight, and they followed him.

### Mark 10:46-52

46 And they came to Jericho: and as he went out of Jericho with his disciples and a great number of people, blind Bartimaeus, the son of Timaeus, sat by the highway side begging.
47 And when he heard that it was Jesus of Nazareth, he began to cry out, and say, Jesus, thou son of David, have mercy on me.
48 And many charged him that he should hold his peace: but he cried the more a great deal, Thou son of David, have mercy on me.
49 And Jesus stood still, and commanded him to be called. And they call the blind man, saying unto him, Be of good comfort, rise; he calleth thee.
50 And he, casting away his garment, rose, and came to Jesus.

51 And Jesus answered and said unto him, What wilt thou that I should do unto thee? The blind man said unto him, Lord, that I might receive my sight.

52 And Jesus said unto him, Go thy way; thy faith hath made thee whole. And immediately he received his sight, and followed Jesus in the way.

### Luke 18:35-43

35 And it came to pass, that as he was come nigh unto Jericho, a certain blind man sat by the way side begging:

36 And hearing the multitude pass by, he asked what it meant.

37 And they told him, that Jesus of Nazareth passeth by.

38 And he cried, saying, Jesus, thou son of David, have mercy on me.

39 And they which went before rebuked him, that he should hold his peace: but he cried so much the more, Thou son of David, have mercy on me.

40 And Jesus stood, and commanded him to be brought unto him: and when he was come near, he asked him,

41 Saying, What wilt thou that I shall do unto thee? And he said, Lord, that I may receive my sight.

42 And Jesus said unto him, Receive thy sight: thy faith hath saved thee.

43 And immediately he received his sight, and followed him, glorifying God: and all the people, when they saw it, gave praise unto God.

## 25. People Rose From Dead When Jesus Gave Up His Spirit – and After Jesus' Resurrection

### Matthew 27:50-53

50 Jesus, when he had cried again with a loud voice, yielded up the ghost.

51 And, behold, the veil of the temple was rent in twain from the top to the bottom; and the earth did quake, and the rocks rent;
52 And the graves were opened; and many bodies of the saints which slept arose,
53 And came out of the graves after his resurrection, and went into the holy city, and appeared unto many.

## 26. Jesus Drives Out Evil Spirit from Mad Man in Synagogue in Capernaum

### Mark 1:21-28; Luke 4:31-37

### Mark 1:21-28

21 And they went into Capernaum; and straightway on the sabbath day he entered into the synagogue, and taught.
22 And they were astonished at his doctrine: for he taught them as one that had authority, and not as the scribes.
23 And there was in their synagogue a man with an unclean spirit; and he cried out,
24 Saying, Let us alone; what have we to do with thee, thou Jesus of Nazareth? art thou come to destroy us? I know thee who thou art, the Holy One of God.
25 And Jesus rebuked him, saying, Hold thy peace, and come out of him.
26 And when the unclean spirit had torn him, and cried with a loud voice, he came out of him.
27 And they were all amazed, insomuch that they questioned among themselves, saying, What thing is this? what new doctrine is this? for with authority commandeth he even the unclean spirits, and they do obey him.
28 And immediately his fame spread abroad throughout all the region round about Galilee.

Healing Examples From The New Testament: The Gospels

## Luke 4:31-37

³¹ And came down to Capernaum, a city of Galilee, and taught them on the sabbath days.
³² And they were astonished at his doctrine: for his word was with power.
³³ And in the synagogue there was a man, which had a spirit of an unclean devil, and cried out with a loud voice,
³⁴ Saying, Let us alone; what have we to do with thee, thou Jesus of Nazareth? art thou come to destroy us? I know thee who thou art; the Holy One of God.
³⁵ And Jesus rebuked him, saying, Hold thy peace, and come out of him. And when the devil had thrown him in the midst, he came out of him, and hurt him not.
³⁶ And they were all amazed, and spake among themselves, saying, What a word is this! for with authority and power he commandeth the unclean spirits, and they come out.
³⁷ And the fame of him went out into every place of the country round about.

## 27. Jesus Appointed Twelve

### Mark 3:13-19

¹³ And he goeth up into a mountain, and calleth unto him whom he would: and they came unto him.
¹⁴ And he ordained twelve, that they should be with him, and that he might send them forth to preach,
¹⁵ And to have power to heal sicknesses, and to cast out devils:
¹⁶ And Simon he surnamed Peter;
¹⁷ And James the son of Zebedee, and John the brother of James; and he surnamed them Boanerges, which is, The sons of thunder:
¹⁸ And Andrew, and Philip, and Bartholomew, and Matthew, and Thomas, and James the son of Alphaeus, and Thaddaeus, and Simon the Canaanite,

19 And Judas Iscariot, which also betrayed him: and they went into an house.

## 28. Jesus Heals Deaf and Dumb Man

### Mark 7:31-37

31 And again, departing from the coasts of Tyre and Sidon, he came unto the sea of Galilee, through the midst of the coasts of Decapolis.
32 And they bring unto him one that was deaf, and had an impediment in his speech; and they beseech him to put his hand upon him.
33 And he took him aside from the multitude, and put his fingers into his ears, and he spit, and touched his tongue;
34 And looking up to heaven, he sighed, and saith unto him, Ephphatha, that is, Be opened.
35 And straightway his ears were opened, and the string of his tongue was loosed, and he spake plain.
36 And he charged them that they should tell no man: but the more he charged them, so much the more a great deal they published it;
37 And were beyond measure astonished, saying, He hath done all things well: he maketh both the deaf to hear, and the dumb to speak.

## 29. Jesus Restores Sight to Blind Man at Bethsaida

### Mark 8:22-26

22 And he cometh to Bethsaida; and they bring a blind man unto him, and besought him to touch him.
23 And he took the blind man by the hand, and led him out of the town; and when he had spit on his eyes, and put his hands upon him, he asked him if he saw ought.
24 And he looked up, and said, I see men as trees, walking.

25 After that he put his hands again upon his eyes, and made him look up: and he was restored, and saw every man clearly.
26 And he sent him away to his house, saying, Neither go into the town, nor tell it to any in the town.

## 30. Man Was Raised From The Dead

There is speculation that this man was raised from the dead.

### Mark 14:51-52

51 And there followed him a certain young man, having a linen cloth cast about his naked body; and the young men laid hold on him:
52 And he left the linen cloth, and fled from them naked.

## 31. Seven Demons Driven from Mary Magdalene (and Other Women)

### Mark 16:9; Luke 8:2

### Mark 16:9

9 Now when Jesus was risen early the first day of the week, he appeared first to Mary Magdalene, out of whom he had cast seven devils.

### Luke 8:2

2 And certain women, which had been healed of evil spirits and infirmities, Mary called Magdalene, out of whom went seven devils

Healing Examples From The New Testament: The Gospels

## 32. Disciples Preach and Work Signs After Jesus' Ascension

### Mark 16:19-20

19 So then after the Lord had spoken unto them, he was received up into heaven, and sat on the right hand of God.
20 And they went forth, and preached every where, the Lord working with them, and confirming the word with signs following. Amen.

## 33. Elizabeth's Womb Restored, John the Baptist Born

### Luke 1:5-25, 41, 57-67

5 There was in the days of Herod, the king of Judaea, a certain priest named Zacharias, of the course of Abia: and his wife was of the daughters of Aaron, and her name was Elisabeth.
6 And they were both righteous before God, walking in all the commandments and ordinances of the Lord blameless.
7 And they had no child, because that Elisabeth was barren, and they both were now well stricken in years.
8 And it came to pass, that while he executed the priest's office before God in the order of his course,
9 According to the custom of the priest's office, his lot was to burn incense when he went into the temple of the Lord.
10 And the whole multitude of the people were praying without at the time of incense.
11 And there appeared unto him an angel of the Lord standing on the right side of the altar of incense.
12 And when Zacharias saw him, he was troubled, and fear fell upon him.
13 But the angel said unto him, Fear not, Zacharias: for thy prayer is heard; and thy wife Elisabeth shall bear thee a son, and thou shalt call his name John.

## Healing Examples From The New Testament: The Gospels

¹⁴ And thou shalt have joy and gladness; and many shall rejoice at his birth.
¹⁵ For he shall be great in the sight of the Lord, and shall drink neither wine nor strong drink; and he shall be filled with the Holy Ghost, even from his mother's womb.
¹⁶ And many of the children of Israel shall he turn to the Lord their God.
¹⁷ And he shall go before him in the spirit and power of Elias, to turn the hearts of the fathers to the children, and the disobedient to the wisdom of the just; to make ready a people prepared for the Lord.
¹⁸ And Zacharias said unto the angel, Whereby shall I know this? for I am an old man, and my wife well stricken in years.
¹⁹ And the angel answering said unto him, I am Gabriel, that stand in the presence of God; and am sent to speak unto thee, and to shew thee these glad tidings.
²⁰ And, behold, thou shalt be dumb, and not able to speak, until the day that these things shall be performed, because thou believest not my words, which shall be fulfilled in their season.
²¹ And the people waited for Zacharias, and marvelled that he tarried so long in the temple.
²² And when he came out, he could not speak unto them: and they perceived that he had seen a vision in the temple: for he beckoned unto them, and remained speechless.
²³ And it came to pass, that, as soon as the days of his ministration were accomplished, he departed to his own house.
²⁴ And after those days his wife Elisabeth conceived, and hid herself five months, saying,
²⁵ Thus hath the Lord dealt with me in the days wherein he looked on me, to take away my reproach among men.

⁴¹ And it came to pass, that, when Elisabeth heard the salutation of Mary, the babe leaped in her womb; and Elisabeth was filled with the Holy Ghost:

## Healing Examples From The New Testament: The Gospels

57 Now Elisabeth's full time came that she should be delivered; and she brought forth a son.
58 And her neighbours and her cousins heard how the Lord had shewed great mercy upon her; and they rejoiced with her.
59 And it came to pass, that on the eighth day they came to circumcise the child; and they called him Zacharias, after the name of his father.
60 And his mother answered and said, Not so; but he shall be called John.
61 And they said unto her, There is none of thy kindred that is called by this name.
62 And they made signs to his father, how he would have him called.
63 And he asked for a writing table, and wrote, saying, His name is John. And they marvelled all.
64 And his mouth was opened immediately, and his tongue loosed, and he spake, and praised God.
65 And fear came on all that dwelt round about them: and all these sayings were noised abroad throughout all the hill country of Judaea.
66 And all they that heard them laid them up in their hearts, saying, What manner of child shall this be! And the hand of the Lord was with him.
67 And his father Zacharias was filled with the Holy Ghost, and prophesied, saying,

## 34. Jesus Raises Widow's Dead Son at Nain

### Luke 7:11-17

11 And it came to pass the day after, that he went into a city called Nain; and many of his disciples went with him, and much people.
12 Now when he came nigh to the gate of the city, behold, there was a dead man carried out, the only son of his

mother, and she was a widow: and much people of the city was with her.

¹³ And when the Lord saw her, he had compassion on her, and said unto her, Weep not.

¹⁴ And he came and touched the bier: and they that bare him stood still. And he said, Young man, I say unto thee, Arise.

¹⁵ And he that was dead sat up, and began to speak. And he delivered him to his mother.

¹⁶ And there came a fear on all: and they glorified God, saying, That a great prophet is risen up among us; and, That God hath visited his people.

¹⁷ And this rumour of him went forth throughout all Judaea, and throughout all the region round about.

## 35. Jesus Sent Out the Seventy-Two

### Luke 10:1, 8-9, 17-20

¹ After these things the Lord appointed other seventy also, and sent them two and two before his face into every city and place, whither he himself would come.

⁸ And into whatsoever city ye enter, and they receive you, eat such things as are set before you:

⁹ And heal the sick that are therein, and say unto them, The kingdom of God is come nigh unto you.

¹⁷ And the seventy returned again with joy, saying, Lord, even the devils are subject unto us through thy name.

¹⁸ And he said unto them, I beheld Satan as lightning fall from heaven.

¹⁹ Behold, I give unto you power to tread on serpents and scorpions, and over all the power of the enemy: and nothing shall by any means hurt you.

²⁰ Notwithstanding in this rejoice not, that the spirits are subject unto you; but rather rejoice, because your names are written in heaven.

Healing Examples From The New Testament: The Gospels

## 36. Jesus Heals Woman Crippled For 18 Years (on the Sabbath)

### Luke 13:10-17

10 And he was teaching in one of the synagogues on the sabbath.
11 And, behold, there was a woman which had a spirit of infirmity eighteen years, and was bowed together, and could in no wise lift up herself.
12 And when Jesus saw her, he called her to him, and said unto her, Woman, thou art loosed from thine infirmity.
13 And he laid his hands on her: and immediately she was made straight, and glorified God.
14 And the ruler of the synagogue answered with indignation, because that Jesus had healed on the sabbath day, and said unto the people, There are six days in which men ought to work: in them therefore come and be healed, and not on the sabbath day.
15 The Lord then answered him, and said, Thou hypocrite, doth not each one of you on the sabbath loose his ox or his ass from the stall, and lead him away to watering?
16 And ought not this woman, being a daughter of Abraham, whom Satan hath bound, lo, these eighteen years, be loosed from this bond on the sabbath day?
17 And when he had said these things, all his adversaries were ashamed: and all the people rejoiced for all the glorious things that were done by him.

## 37. Jesus Heals Man With Dropsy (on the Sabbath)

### Luke 14:1-6

1 And it came to pass, as he went into the house of one of the chief Pharisees to eat bread on the sabbath day, that they watched him.

2 And, behold, there was a certain man before him which had the dropsy.
3 And Jesus answering spake unto the lawyers and Pharisees, saying, Is it lawful to heal on the sabbath day?
4 And they held their peace. And he took him, and healed him, and let him go;
5 And answered them, saying, Which of you shall have an ass or an ox fallen into a pit, and will not straightway pull him out on the sabbath day?
6 And they could not answer him again to these things.

## 38. Jesus Cleanses Ten Leprous Men

### Luke 17:11-19

11 And it came to pass, as he went to Jerusalem, that he passed through the midst of Samaria and Galilee.
12 And as he entered into a certain village, there met him ten men that were lepers, which stood afar off:
13 And they lifted up their voices, and said, Jesus, Master, have mercy on us.
14 And when he saw them, he said unto them, Go shew yourselves unto the priests. And it came to pass, that, as they went, they were cleansed.
15 And one of them, when he saw that he was healed, turned back, and with a loud voice glorified God,
16 And fell down on his face at his feet, giving him thanks: and he was a Samaritan.
17 And Jesus answering said, Were there not ten cleansed? but where are the nine?
18 There are not found that returned to give glory to God, save this stranger.
19 And he said unto him, Arise, go thy way: thy faith hath made thee whole.

Healing Examples From The New Testament: The Gospels

# 39. Jesus Restores Malchus' Ear at Gethsemane

## Luke 22:47-51; John 18:11

### Luke 22:47-51

47 And while he yet spake, behold a multitude, and he that was called Judas, one of the twelve, went before them, and drew near unto Jesus to kiss him.
48 But Jesus said unto him, Judas, betrayest thou the Son of man with a kiss?
49 When they which were about him saw what would follow, they said unto him, Lord, shall we smite with the sword?
50 And one of them smote the servant of the high priest, and cut off his right ear.
51 And Jesus answered and said, Suffer ye thus far. And he touched his ear, and healed him.

### John 18:1-11

1 When Jesus had spoken these words, he went forth with his disciples over the brook Cedron, where was a garden, into the which he entered, and his disciples.
2 And Judas also, which betrayed him, knew the place: for Jesus ofttimes resorted thither with his disciples.
3 Judas then, having received a band of men and officers from the chief priests and Pharisees, cometh thither with lanterns and torches and weapons.
4 Jesus therefore, knowing all things that should come upon him, went forth, and said unto them, Whom seek ye?
5 They answered him, Jesus of Nazareth. Jesus saith unto them, I am he. And Judas also, which betrayed him, stood with them.
6 As soon then as he had said unto them, I am he, they went backward, and fell to the ground.
7 Then asked he them again, Whom seek ye? And they said, Jesus of Nazareth.
8 Jesus answered, I have told you that I am he: if therefore ye seek me, let these go their way:

9 That the saying might be fulfilled, which he spake, Of them which thou gavest me have I lost none.

10 Then Simon Peter having a sword drew it, and smote the high priest's servant, and cut off his right ear. The servant's name was Malchus.

11 Then said Jesus unto Peter, Put up thy sword into the sheath: the cup which my Father hath given me, shall I not drink it?

## 40. Jesus Heals Royal Official's Son

### John 4:43-54

43 Now after two days he departed thence, and went into Galilee.

44 For Jesus himself testified, that a prophet hath no honour in his own country.

45 Then when he was come into Galilee, the Galilaeans received him, having seen all the things that he did at Jerusalem at the feast: for they also went unto the feast.

46 So Jesus came again into Cana of Galilee, where he made the water wine. And there was a certain nobleman, whose son was sick at Capernaum.

47 When he heard that Jesus was come out of Judaea into Galilee, he went unto him, and besought him that he would come down, and heal his son: for he was at the point of death.

48 Then said Jesus unto him, Except ye see signs and wonders, ye will not believe.

49 The nobleman saith unto him, Sir, come down ere my child die.

50 Jesus saith unto him, Go thy way; thy son liveth. And the man believed the word that Jesus had spoken unto him, and he went his way.

51 And as he was now going down, his servants met him, and told him, saying, Thy son liveth.

52 Then enquired he of them the hour when he began to amend. And they said unto him, Yesterday at the seventh hour the fever left him.
53 So the father knew that it was at the same hour, in the which Jesus said unto him, Thy son liveth: and himself believed, and his whole house.
54 This is again the second miracle that Jesus did, when he was come out of Judaea into Galilee.

## 41. Jesus Heals the Invalid at Pool of Bethsaida

### John 5:1-15

1 After this there was a feast of the Jews; and Jesus went up to Jerusalem.
2 Now there is at Jerusalem by the sheep market a pool, which is called in the Hebrew tongue Bethesda, having five porches.
3 In these lay a great multitude of impotent folk, of blind, halt, withered, waiting for the moving of the water.
4 For an angel went down at a certain season into the pool, and troubled the water: whosoever then first after the troubling of the water stepped in was made whole of whatsoever disease he had.
5 And a certain man was there, which had an infirmity thirty and eight years.
6 When Jesus saw him lie, and knew that he had been now a long time in that case, he saith unto him, Wilt thou be made whole?
7 The impotent man answered him, Sir, I have no man, when the water is troubled, to put me into the pool: but while I am coming, another steppeth down before me.
8 Jesus saith unto him, Rise, take up thy bed, and walk.
9 And immediately the man was made whole, and took up his bed, and walked: and on the same day was the sabbath.
10 The Jews therefore said unto him that was cured, It is the sabbath day: it is not lawful for thee to carry thy bed.

¹¹ He answered them, He that made me whole, the same said unto me, Take up thy bed, and walk.
¹² Then asked they him, What man is that which said unto thee, Take up thy bed, and walk?
13 And he that was healed wist not who it was: for Jesus had conveyed himself away, a multitude being in that place.
¹⁴ Afterward Jesus findeth him in the temple, and said unto him, Behold, thou art made whole: sin no more, lest a worse thing come unto thee.
¹⁵ The man departed, and told the Jews that it was Jesus, which had made him whole.

## 42. Jesus Heals Man Born Blind

### John 9:1-12

¹ And as Jesus passed by, he saw a man which was blind from his birth.
² And his disciples asked him, saying, Master, who did sin, this man, or his parents, that he was born blind?
³ Jesus answered, Neither hath this man sinned, nor his parents: but that the works of God should be made manifest in him.
⁴ I must work the works of him that sent me, while it is day: the night cometh, when no man can work.
⁵ As long as I am in the world, I am the light of the world.
⁶ When he had thus spoken, he spat on the ground, and made clay of the spittle, and he anointed the eyes of the blind man with the clay,
⁷ And said unto him, Go, wash in the pool of Siloam, (which is by interpretation, Sent.) He went his way therefore, and washed, and came seeing.
⁸ The neighbours therefore, and they which before had seen him that he was blind, said, Is not this he that sat and begged?
⁹ Some said, This is he: others said, He is like him: but he said, I am he.

10 Therefore said they unto him, How were thine eyes opened?
11 He answered and said, A man that is called Jesus made clay, and anointed mine eyes, and said unto me, Go to the pool of Siloam, and wash: and I went and washed, and I received sight.
12 Then said they unto him, Where is he? He said, I know not.

## 43. Jesus Raises Lazarus From the Dead

### John 11:1-45

1 Now a certain man was sick, named Lazarus, of Bethany, the town of Mary and her sister Martha.
2 (It was that Mary which anointed the Lord with ointment, and wiped his feet with her hair, whose brother Lazarus was sick.)
3 Therefore his sisters sent unto him, saying, Lord, behold, he whom thou lovest is sick.
4 When Jesus heard that, he said, This sickness is not unto death, but for the glory of God, that the Son of God might be glorified thereby.
5 Now Jesus loved Martha, and her sister, and Lazarus.
6 When he had heard therefore that he was sick, he abode two days still in the same place where he was.
7 Then after that saith he to his disciples, Let us go into Judaea again.
8 His disciples say unto him, Master, the Jews of late sought to stone thee; and goest thou thither again?
9 Jesus answered, Are there not twelve hours in the day? If any man walk in the day, he stumbleth not, because he seeth the light of this world.
10 But if a man walk in the night, he stumbleth, because there is no light in him.

## Healing Examples From The New Testament: The Gospels

¹¹ These things said he: and after that he saith unto them, Our friend Lazarus sleepeth; but I go, that I may awake him out of sleep.

¹² Then said his disciples, Lord, if he sleep, he shall do well.

¹³ Howbeit Jesus spake of his death: but they thought that he had spoken of taking of rest in sleep.

¹⁴ Then said Jesus unto them plainly, Lazarus is dead.

¹⁵ And I am glad for your sakes that I was not there, to the intent ye may believe; nevertheless let us go unto him.

¹⁶ Then said Thomas, which is called Didymus, unto his fellowdisciples, Let us also go, that we may die with him.

¹⁷ Then when Jesus came, he found that he had lain in the grave four days already.

¹⁸ Now Bethany was nigh unto Jerusalem, about fifteen furlongs off:

¹⁹ And many of the Jews came to Martha and Mary, to comfort them concerning their brother.

²⁰ Then Martha, as soon as she heard that Jesus was coming, went and met him: but Mary sat still in the house.

²¹ Then said Martha unto Jesus, Lord, if thou hadst been here, my brother had not died.

²² But I know, that even now, whatsoever thou wilt ask of God, God will give it thee.

²³ Jesus saith unto her, Thy brother shall rise again.

²⁴ Martha saith unto him, I know that he shall rise again in the resurrection at the last day.

²⁵ Jesus said unto her, I am the resurrection, and the life: he that believeth in me, though he were dead, yet shall he live:

²⁶ And whosoever liveth and believeth in me shall never die. Believest thou this?

²⁷ She saith unto him, Yea, Lord: I believe that thou art the Christ, the Son of God, which should come into the world.

²⁸ And when she had so said, she went her way, and called Mary her sister secretly, saying, The Master is come, and calleth for thee.

²⁹ As soon as she heard that, she arose quickly, and came unto him.

30 Now Jesus was not yet come into the town, but was in that place where Martha met him.

31 The Jews then which were with her in the house, and comforted her, when they saw Mary, that she rose up hastily and went out, followed her, saying, She goeth unto the grave to weep there.

32 Then when Mary was come where Jesus was, and saw him, she fell down at his feet, saying unto him, Lord, if thou hadst been here, my brother had not died.

33 When Jesus therefore saw her weeping, and the Jews also weeping which came with her, he groaned in the spirit, and was troubled.

34 And said, Where have ye laid him? They said unto him, Lord, come and see.

35 Jesus wept.

36 Then said the Jews, Behold how he loved him!

37 And some of them said, Could not this man, which opened the eyes of the blind, have caused that even this man should not have died?

38 Jesus therefore again groaning in himself cometh to the grave. It was a cave, and a stone lay upon it.

39 Jesus said, Take ye away the stone. Martha, the sister of him that was dead, saith unto him, Lord, by this time he stinketh: for he hath been dead four days.

40 Jesus saith unto her, Said I not unto thee, that, if thou wouldest believe, thou shouldest see the glory of God?

41 Then they took away the stone from the place where the dead was laid. And Jesus lifted up his eyes, and said, Father, I thank thee that thou hast heard me.

42 And I knew that thou hearest me always: but because of the people which stand by I said it, that they may believe that thou hast sent me.

43 And when he thus had spoken, he cried with a loud voice, Lazarus, come forth.

44 And he that was dead came forth, bound hand and foot with graveclothes: and his face was bound about with a napkin. Jesus saith unto them, Loose him, and let him go.

45 Then many of the Jews which came to Mary, and had seen the things which Jesus did, believed on him.

## 44. Jesus Is Resurrected from the Dead

### Matthew 15:1-20; Mark 16:1-20; Luke 24:1-53; John 20:1-31

### Matthew 15:1-20

1 In the end of the sabbath, as it began to dawn toward the first day of the week, came Mary Magdalene and the other Mary to see the sepulchre.
2 And, behold, there was a great earthquake: for the angel of the Lord descended from heaven, and came and rolled back the stone from the door, and sat upon it.
3 His countenance was like lightning, and his raiment white as snow:
4 And for fear of him the keepers did shake, and became as dead men.
5 And the angel answered and said unto the women, Fear not ye: for I know that ye seek Jesus, which was crucified.
6 He is not here: for he is risen, as he said. Come, see the place where the Lord lay.
7 And go quickly, and tell his disciples that he is risen from the dead; and, behold, he goeth before you into Galilee; there shall ye see him: lo, I have told you.
8 And they departed quickly from the sepulchre with fear and great joy; and did run to bring his disciples word.
9 And as they went to tell his disciples, behold, Jesus met them, saying, All hail. And they came and held him by the feet, and worshipped him.
10 Then said Jesus unto them, Be not afraid: go tell my brethren that they go into Galilee, and there shall they see me.
11 Now when they were going, behold, some of the watch came into the city, and shewed unto the chief priests all the things that were done.

## Healing Examples From The New Testament: The Gospels

12 And when they were assembled with the elders, and had taken counsel, they gave large money unto the soldiers,
13 Saying, Say ye, His disciples came by night, and stole him away while we slept.
14 And if this come to the governor's ears, we will persuade him, and secure you.
15 So they took the money, and did as they were taught: and this saying is commonly reported among the Jews until this day.
16 Then the eleven disciples went away into Galilee, into a mountain where Jesus had appointed them.
17 And when they saw him, they worshipped him: but some doubted.
18 And Jesus came and spake unto them, saying, All power is given unto me in heaven and in earth.
19 Go ye therefore, and teach all nations, baptizing them in the name of the Father, and of the Son, and of the Holy Ghost:
20 Teaching them to observe all things whatsoever I have commanded you: and, lo, I am with you always, even unto the end of the world. Amen.

## Mark 16:1-20

1 And when the sabbath was past, Mary Magdalene, and Mary the mother of James, and Salome, had bought sweet spices, that they might come and anoint him.
2 And very early in the morning the first day of the week, they came unto the sepulchre at the rising of the sun.
3 And they said among themselves, Who shall roll us away the stone from the door of the sepulchre?
4 And when they looked, they saw that the stone was rolled away: for it was very great.
5 And entering into the sepulchre, they saw a young man sitting on the right side, clothed in a long white garment; and they were affrighted.

## Healing Examples From The New Testament: The Gospels

⁶ And he saith unto them, Be not affrighted: Ye seek Jesus of Nazareth, which was crucified: he is risen; he is not here: behold the place where they laid him.

⁷ But go your way, tell his disciples and Peter that he goeth before you into Galilee: there shall ye see him, as he said unto you.

⁸ And they went out quickly, and fled from the sepulchre; for they trembled and were amazed: neither said they any thing to any man; for they were afraid.

⁹ Now when Jesus was risen early the first day of the week, he appeared first to Mary Magdalene, out of whom he had cast seven devils.

¹⁰ And she went and told them that had been with him, as they mourned and wept.

¹¹ And they, when they had heard that he was alive, and had been seen of her, believed not.

¹² After that he appeared in another form unto two of them, as they walked, and went into the country.

¹³ And they went and told it unto the residue: neither believed they them.

¹⁴ Afterward he appeared unto the eleven as they sat at meat, and upbraided them with their unbelief and hardness of heart, because they believed not them which had seen him after he was risen.

¹⁵ And he said unto them, Go ye into all the world, and preach the gospel to every creature.

¹⁶ He that believeth and is baptized shall be saved; but he that believeth not shall be damned.

¹⁷ And these signs shall follow them that believe; In my name shall they cast out devils; they shall speak with new tongues;

¹⁸ They shall take up serpents; and if they drink any deadly thing, it shall not hurt them; they shall lay hands on the sick, and they shall recover.

¹⁹ So then after the Lord had spoken unto them, he was received up into heaven, and sat on the right hand of God.

20 And they went forth, and preached every where, the Lord working with them, and confirming the word with signs following. Amen.

## Luke 24:1-53

1 Now upon the first day of the week, very early in the morning, they came unto the sepulchre, bringing the spices which they had prepared, and certain others with them.
2 And they found the stone rolled away from the sepulchre.
3 And they entered in, and found not the body of the Lord Jesus.
4 And it came to pass, as they were much perplexed thereabout, behold, two men stood by them in shining garments:
5 And as they were afraid, and bowed down their faces to the earth, they said unto them, Why seek ye the living among the dead?
6 He is not here, but is risen: remember how he spake unto you when he was yet in Galilee,
7 Saying, The Son of man must be delivered into the hands of sinful men, and be crucified, and the third day rise again.
8 And they remembered his words,
9 And returned from the sepulchre, and told all these things unto the eleven, and to all the rest.
10 It was Mary Magdalene and Joanna, and Mary the mother of James, and other women that were with them, which told these things unto the apostles.
11 And their words seemed to them as idle tales, and they believed them not.
12 Then arose Peter, and ran unto the sepulchre; and stooping down, he beheld the linen clothes laid by themselves, and departed, wondering in himself at that which was come to pass.
13 And, behold, two of them went that same day to a village called Emmaus, which was from Jerusalem about threescore furlongs.

## Healing Examples From The New Testament: The Gospels

¹⁴ And they talked together of all these things which had happened.

¹⁵ And it came to pass, that, while they communed together and reasoned, Jesus himself drew near, and went with them.

¹⁶ But their eyes were holden that they should not know him.

¹⁷ And he said unto them, What manner of communications are these that ye have one to another, as ye walk, and are sad?

¹⁸ And the one of them, whose name was Cleopas, answering said unto him, Art thou only a stranger in Jerusalem, and hast not known the things which are come to pass there in these days?

¹⁹ And he said unto them, What things? And they said unto him, Concerning Jesus of Nazareth, which was a prophet mighty in deed and word before God and all the people:

²⁰ And how the chief priests and our rulers delivered him to be condemned to death, and have crucified him.

²¹ But we trusted that it had been he which should have redeemed Israel: and beside all this, to day is the third day since these things were done.

²² Yea, and certain women also of our company made us astonished, which were early at the sepulchre;

²³ And when they found not his body, they came, saying, that they had also seen a vision of angels, which said that he was alive.

²⁴ And certain of them which were with us went to the sepulchre, and found it even so as the women had said: but him they saw not.

²⁵ Then he said unto them, O fools, and slow of heart to believe all that the prophets have spoken:

²⁶ Ought not Christ to have suffered these things, and to enter into his glory?

²⁷ And beginning at Moses and all the prophets, he expounded unto them in all the scriptures the things concerning himself.

²⁸ And they drew nigh unto the village, whither they went: and he made as though he would have gone further.

29 But they constrained him, saying, Abide with us: for it is toward evening, and the day is far spent. And he went in to tarry with them.

30 And it came to pass, as he sat at meat with them, he took bread, and blessed it, and brake, and gave to them.

31 And their eyes were opened, and they knew him; and he vanished out of their sight.

32 And they said one to another, Did not our heart burn within us, while he talked with us by the way, and while he opened to us the scriptures?

33 And they rose up the same hour, and returned to Jerusalem, and found the eleven gathered together, and them that were with them,

34 Saying, The Lord is risen indeed, and hath appeared to Simon.

35 And they told what things were done in the way, and how he was known of them in breaking of bread.

36 And as they thus spake, Jesus himself stood in the midst of them, and saith unto them, Peace be unto you.

37 But they were terrified and affrighted, and supposed that they had seen a spirit.

38 And he said unto them, Why are ye troubled? and why do thoughts arise in your hearts?

39 Behold my hands and my feet, that it is I myself: handle me, and see; for a spirit hath not flesh and bones, as ye see me have.

40 And when he had thus spoken, he shewed them his hands and his feet.

41 And while they yet believed not for joy, and wondered, he said unto them, Have ye here any meat?

42 And they gave him a piece of a broiled fish, and of an honeycomb.

43 And he took it, and did eat before them.

44 And he said unto them, These are the words which I spake unto you, while I was yet with you, that all things must be fulfilled, which were written in the law of Moses, and in the prophets, and in the psalms, concerning me.

## Healing Examples From The New Testament: The Gospels

⁴⁵ Then opened he their understanding, that they might understand the scriptures,
⁴⁶ And said unto them, Thus it is written, and thus it behooved Christ to suffer, and to rise from the dead the third day:
⁴⁷ And that repentance and remission of sins should be preached in his name among all nations, beginning at Jerusalem.
⁴⁸ And ye are witnesses of these things.
⁴⁹ And, behold, I send the promise of my Father upon you: but tarry ye in the city of Jerusalem, until ye be endued with power from on high.
⁵⁰ And he led them out as far as to Bethany, and he lifted up his hands, and blessed them.
⁵¹ And it came to pass, while he blessed them, he was parted from them, and carried up into heaven.
⁵² And they worshipped him, and returned to Jerusalem with great joy:
⁵³ And were continually in the temple, praising and blessing God. Amen.

## John 20:1-31

¹ The first day of the week cometh Mary Magdalene early, when it was yet dark, unto the sepulchre, and seeth the stone taken away from the sepulchre.
² Then she runneth, and cometh to Simon Peter, and to the other disciple, whom Jesus loved, and saith unto them, They have taken away the Lord out of the sepulchre, and we know not where they have laid him.
³ Peter therefore went forth, and that other disciple, and came to the sepulchre.
⁴ So they ran both together: and the other disciple did outrun Peter, and came first to the sepulchre.
⁵ And he stooping down, and looking in, saw the linen clothes lying; yet went he not in.
⁶ Then cometh Simon Peter following him, and went into the sepulchre, and seeth the linen clothes lie,

7 And the napkin, that was about his head, not lying with the linen clothes, but wrapped together in a place by itself.

8 Then went in also that other disciple, which came first to the sepulchre, and he saw, and believed.

9 For as yet they knew not the scripture, that he must rise again from the dead.

10 Then the disciples went away again unto their own home.

11 But Mary stood without at the sepulchre weeping: and as she wept, she stooped down, and looked into the sepulchre,

12 And seeth two angels in white sitting, the one at the head, and the other at the feet, where the body of Jesus had lain.

13 And they say unto her, Woman, why weepest thou? She saith unto them, Because they have taken away my Lord, and I know not where they have laid him.

14 And when she had thus said, she turned herself back, and saw Jesus standing, and knew not that it was Jesus.

15 Jesus saith unto her, Woman, why weepest thou? whom seekest thou? She, supposing him to be the gardener, saith unto him, Sir, if thou have borne him hence, tell me where thou hast laid him, and I will take him away.

16 Jesus saith unto her, Mary. She turned herself, and saith unto him, Rabboni; which is to say, Master.

17 Jesus saith unto her, Touch me not; for I am not yet ascended to my Father: but go to my brethren, and say unto them, I ascend unto my Father, and your Father; and to my God, and your God.

18 Mary Magdalene came and told the disciples that she had seen the Lord, and that he had spoken these things unto her.

19 Then the same day at evening, being the first day of the week, when the doors were shut where the disciples were assembled for fear of the Jews, came Jesus and stood in the midst, and saith unto them, Peace be unto you.

20 And when he had so said, he shewed unto them his hands and his side. Then were the disciples glad, when they saw the Lord.

## Healing Examples From The New Testament: The Gospels

21 Then said Jesus to them again, Peace be unto you: as my Father hath sent me, even so send I you.

22 And when he had said this, he breathed on them, and saith unto them, Receive ye the Holy Ghost:

23 Whose soever sins ye remit, they are remitted unto them; and whose soever sins ye retain, they are retained.

24 But Thomas, one of the twelve, called Didymus, was not with them when Jesus came.

25 The other disciples therefore said unto him, We have seen the Lord. But he said unto them, Except I shall see in his hands the print of the nails, and put my finger into the print of the nails, and thrust my hand into his side, I will not believe.

26 And after eight days again his disciples were within, and Thomas with them: then came Jesus, the doors being shut, and stood in the midst, and said, Peace be unto you.

27 Then saith he to Thomas, Reach hither thy finger, and behold my hands; and reach hither thy hand, and thrust it into my side: and be not faithless, but believing.

28 And Thomas answered and said unto him, My Lord and my God.

29 Jesus saith unto him, Thomas, because thou hast seen me, thou hast believed: blessed are they that have not seen, and yet have believed.

30 And many other signs truly did Jesus in the presence of his disciples, which are not written in this book:

31 But these are written, that ye might believe that Jesus is the Christ, the Son of God; and that believing ye might have life through his name.

# Healing Examples From The New Testament: The Book of Acts and The Epistles

## 1.  Man at the Gate of Beautiful Healed (Peter with John)

### Acts 3:1-11

¹ Now Peter and John went up together into the temple at the hour of prayer, being the ninth hour.
² And a certain man lame from his mother's womb was carried, whom they laid daily at the gate of the temple which is called Beautiful, to ask alms of them that entered into the temple;
³ Who seeing Peter and John about to go into the temple asked an alms.
⁴ And Peter, fastening his eyes upon him with John, said, Look on us.
⁵ And he gave heed unto them, expecting to receive something of them.
⁶ Then Peter said, Silver and gold have I none; but such as I have give I thee: In the name of Jesus Christ of Nazareth rise up and walk.
⁷ And he took him by the right hand, and lifted him up: and immediately his feet and ankle bones received strength.
⁸ And he leaping up stood, and walked, and entered with them into the temple, walking, and leaping, and praising God.
⁹ And all the people saw him walking and praising God:
¹⁰ And they knew that it was he which sat for alms at the Beautiful gate of the temple: and they were filled with

Healing Examples From The New Testament: Acts and the Epistles

wonder and amazement at that which had happened unto him.
[11] And as the lame man which was healed held Peter and John, all the people ran together unto them in the porch that is called Solomon's, greatly wondering.

## 2. Apostles Stretched For Their Hands To Heal

### Acts 4:29-30

[29] And now, Lord, behold their threatenings: and grant unto thy servants, that with all boldness they may speak thy word,
[30] By stretching forth thine hand to heal; and that signs and wonders may be done by the name of thy holy child Jesus.

## 3. Apostles Do Signs and Wonders, People Healed Who Fell Under Peter's Shadow

### Acts 5:12-16

[12] And by the hands of the apostles were many signs and wonders wrought among the people; (and they were all with one accord in Solomon's porch.
[13] And of the rest durst no man join himself to them: but the people magnified them.
[14] And believers were the more added to the Lord, multitudes both of men and women.)
[15] Insomuch that they brought forth the sick into the streets, and laid them on beds and couches, that at the least the shadow of Peter passing by might overshadow some of them.
[16] There came also a multitude out of the cities round about unto Jerusalem, bringing sick folks, and them which were vexed with unclean spirits: and they were healed every one.

Healing Examples From The New Testament: Acts and the Epistles

## 4. Great Wonders and Miracles Through Stephen

### Acts 6:8

8 And Stephen, full of faith and power, did great wonders and miracles among the people

## 5. Phillip's Mission Included Healing

### Acts 8:4-8

4 Therefore they that were scattered abroad went every where preaching the word.
5 Then Philip went down to the city of Samaria, and preached Christ unto them.
6 And the people with one accord gave heed unto those things which Philip spake, hearing and seeing the miracles which he did.
7 For unclean spirits, crying with loud voice, came out of many that were possessed with them: and many taken with palsies, and that were lame, were healed.
8 And there was great joy in that city.

## 6. Ananias Laid Hands on Saul (Paul), His Sight Restored

### Acts 9:8-10, 17-20

8 And Saul arose from the earth; and when his eyes were opened, he saw no man: but they led him by the hand, and brought him into Damascus.
9 And he was three days without sight, and neither did eat nor drink.
10 And there was a certain disciple at Damascus, named Ananias; and to him said the Lord in a vision, Ananias. And he said, Behold, I am here, Lord.

17 And Ananias went his way, and entered into the house; and putting his hands on him said, Brother Saul, the Lord, even Jesus, that appeared unto thee in the way as thou camest, hath sent me, that thou mightest receive thy sight, and be filled with the Holy Ghost.
18 And immediately there fell from his eyes as it had been scales: and he received sight forthwith, and arose, and was baptized.
19 And when he had received meat, he was strengthened. Then was Saul certain days with the disciples which were at Damascus.
20 And straightway he preached Christ in the synagogues, that he is the Son of God.

## 7. Aeneas Healed of Palsy (Paralysis) (Peter)

### Acts 9:32-35

32 And it came to pass, as Peter passed throughout all quarters, he came down also to the saints which dwelt at Lydda.
33 And there he found a certain man named Aeneas, which had kept his bed eight years, and was sick of the palsy.
34 And Peter said unto him, Aeneas, Jesus Christ maketh thee whole: arise, and make thy bed. And he arose immediately.
35 And all that dwelt at Lydda and Saron saw him, and turned to the Lord.

## 8. Tabitha (Dorcas) Raised From Death To Life (Peter)

### Acts 9:36-42

36 Now there was at Joppa a certain disciple named Tabitha, which by interpretation is called Dorcas: this woman was full of good works and almsdeeds which she did.

37 And it came to pass in those days, that she was sick, and died: whom when they had washed, they laid her in an upper chamber.

38 And forasmuch as Lydda was nigh to Joppa, and the disciples had heard that Peter was there, they sent unto him two men, desiring him that he would not delay to come to them.

39 Then Peter arose and went with them. When he was come, they brought him into the upper chamber: and all the widows stood by him weeping, and shewing the coats and garments which Dorcas made, while she was with them.

40 But Peter put them all forth, and kneeled down, and prayed; and turning him to the body said, Tabitha, arise. And she opened her eyes: and when she saw Peter, she sat up.

41 And he gave her his hand, and lifted her up, and when he had called the saints and widows, presented her alive.

42 And it was known throughout all Joppa; and many believed in the Lord.

## 9. Jesus Healed All That Were Possessed of The Devil

### Acts 10:38

38 How God anointed Jesus of Nazareth with the Holy Ghost and with power: who went about doing good, and healing all that were oppressed of the devil; for God was with him.

Healing Examples From The New Testament: Acts and the Epistles

## 10. In Iconium, God Confirmed His Word Through Signs & Wonders by Paul and Barnabas

### Acts 14:3; Acts 15:12; Romans 15:19

### Acts 14:3

3 Long time therefore abode they speaking boldly in the Lord, which gave testimony unto the word of his grace, and granted signs and wonders to be done by their hands.

### Acts 15:12

12 Then all the multitude kept silence, and gave audience to Barnabas and Paul, declaring what miracles and wonders God had wrought among the Gentiles by them.

### Romans 15:19

19 Through mighty signs and wonders, by the power of the Spirit of God; so that from Jerusalem, and round about unto Illyricum, I have fully preached the gospel of Christ.

## 11. Healing for a Man Lame From Birth at Lystra (Paul)

### Acts 14:8-10

8 And there sat a certain man at Lystra, impotent in his feet, being a cripple from his mother's womb, who never had walked:
9 The same heard Paul speak: who stedfastly beholding him, and perceiving that he had faith to be healed,
10 Said with a loud voice, Stand upright on thy feet. And he leaped and walked.

## 12. Evil Spirit Driven From Damsel (Paul)

### Acts 16:16-18

16 And it came to pass, as we went to prayer, a certain damsel possessed with a spirit of divination met us, which brought her masters much gain by soothsaying:
17 The same followed Paul and us, and cried, saying, These men are the servants of the most high God, which shew unto us the way of salvation.
18 And this did she many days. But Paul, being grieved, turned and said to the spirit, I command thee in the name of Jesus Christ to come out of her. And he came out the same hour.

## 13. People Healed By Paul Sending His Handkerchiefs or Aprons

### Acts 19:11-12

11 And God wrought special miracles by the hands of Paul:
12 So that from his body were brought unto the sick handkerchiefs or aprons, and the diseases departed from them, and the evil spirits went out of them.

## 14. Sons of Sceva Failed to Drive Out Evil Spirit

### Acts 19:13-19

13 Then certain of the vagabond Jews, exorcists, took upon them to call over them which had evil spirits the name of the Lord Jesus, saying, We adjure you by Jesus whom Paul preacheth.
14 And there were seven sons of one Sceva, a Jew, and chief of the priests, which did so.
15 And the evil spirit answered and said, Jesus I know, and Paul I know; but who are ye?

¹⁶ And the man in whom the evil spirit was leaped on them, and overcame them, and prevailed against them, so that they fled out of that house naked and wounded.

¹⁷ And this was known to all the Jews and Greeks also dwelling at Ephesus; and fear fell on them all, and the name of the Lord Jesus was magnified.

¹⁸ And many that believed came, and confessed, and shewed their deeds.

## 15. Eutychus Raised Back to Life (Paul)

### Acts 20:6-12

⁶ And we sailed away from Philippi after the days of unleavened bread, and came unto them to Troas in five days; where we abode seven days.

⁷ And upon the first day of the week, when the disciples came together to break bread, Paul preached unto them, ready to depart on the morrow; and continued his speech until midnight.

⁸ And there were many lights in the upper chamber, where they were gathered together.

⁹ And there sat in a window a certain young man named Eutychus, being fallen into a deep sleep: and as Paul was long preaching, he sunk down with sleep, and fell down from the third loft, and was taken up dead.

¹⁰ And Paul went down, and fell on him, and embracing him said, Trouble not yourselves; for his life is in him.

¹¹ When he therefore was come up again, and had broken bread, and eaten, and talked a long while, even till break of day, so he departed.

¹² And they brought the young man alive, and were not a little comforted.

## 16. Was Paul Healed – Or Raised from the Dead?

### Acts 20:19-20

[19] And there came thither certain Jews from Antioch and Iconium, who persuaded the people, and having stoned Paul, drew him out of the city, supposing he had been dead.
[20] Howbeit, as the disciples stood round about him, he rose up, and came into the city: and the next day he departed with Barnabas to Derbe.

## 17. Paul Exhibits Immunity to Viper's Bite

### Acts 28:1-6

[1] And when they were escaped, then they knew that the island was called Melita.
[2] And the barbarous people shewed us no little kindness: for they kindled a fire, and received us every one, because of the present rain, and because of the cold.
[3] And when Paul had gathered a bundle of sticks, and laid them on the fire, there came a viper out of the heat, and fastened on his hand.
[4] And when the barbarians saw the venomous beast hang on his hand, they said among themselves, No doubt this man is a murderer, whom, though he hath escaped the sea, yet vengeance suffereth not to live.
[5] And he shook off the beast into the fire, and felt no harm.
[6] Howbeit they looked when he should have swollen, or fallen down dead suddenly: but after they had looked a great while, and saw no harm come to him, they changed their minds, and said that he was a god.

Healing Examples From The New Testament: Acts and the Epistles

## 18. Publius' Father Healed of Fever and Bloody Diarrhea (Paul)

### Acts 28:7-8

7 In the same quarters were possessions of the chief man of the island, whose name was Publius; who received us, and lodged us three days courteously.
8 And it came to pass, that the father of Publius lay sick of a fever and of a bloody flux: to whom Paul entered in, and prayed, and laid his hands on him, and healed him.

## 19. Others Healed of Diseases On Island of Malta (Paul)

### Acts 28:9

9 So when this was done, others also, which had diseases in the island, came, and were healed:

## 20. Abraham and Sarah's Bodies Restored Through Faith

### Romans 4:16-22

16 Therefore it is of faith, that it might be by grace; to the end the promise might be sure to all the seed; not to that only which is of the law, but to that also which is of the faith of Abraham; who is the father of us all,
17 (As it is written, I have made thee a father of many nations,) before him whom he believed, even God, who quickeneth the dead, and calleth those things which be not as though they were.
18 Who against hope believed in hope, that he might become the father of many nations, according to that which was spoken, So shall thy seed be.

[19] And being not weak in faith, he considered not his own body now dead, when he was about an hundred years old, neither yet the deadness of Sarah's womb:
[20] He staggered not at the promise of God through unbelief; but was strong in faith, giving glory to God;
[21] And being fully persuaded that, what he had promised, he was able also to perform.
[22] And therefore it was imputed to him for righteousness.

## 21. Sarah Given Strength to Conceive, Abraham's Body Restored

### Hebrews 11:11-12

[11] Through faith also Sara herself received strength to conceive seed, and was delivered of a child when she was past age, because she judged him faithful who had promised.
[12] Therefore sprang there even of one, and him as good as dead, so many as the stars of the sky in multitude, and as the sand which is by the sea shore innumerable.

# Examples of
# Barren Women & Miraculous Births

With the exception of the scriptures on Mary, the Mother of Jesus, all of the scriptures in this section are duplicated in the Old Testament and New Testament examples of healing.

## 1.  Sarah's Womb Restored, Isaac Was Born

### Genesis 17:15-19; 18:10-14; 21:1-8

**Genesis 17:15-19**

17 And God said unto Abraham, As for Sarai thy wife, thou shalt not call her name Sarai, but Sarah shall her name be.
16 And I will bless her, and give thee a son also of her: yea, I will bless her, and she shall be a mother of nations; kings of people shall be of her.
17 Then Abraham fell upon his face, and laughed, and said in his heart, Shall a child be born unto him that is an hundred years old? and shall Sarah, that is ninety years old, bear?
18 And Abraham said unto God, O that Ishmael might live before thee!
19 And God said, Sarah thy wife shall bear thee a son indeed; and thou shalt call his name Isaac: and I will establish my covenant with him for an everlasting covenant, and with his seed after him.

**Genesis 18:9-14**

9 And they said unto him, Where is Sarah thy wife? And he said, Behold, in the tent.
10 And he said, I will certainly return unto thee according to the time of life; and, lo, Sarah thy wife shall have a son. And Sarah heard it in the tent door, which was behind him.

## Examples of Barren Women & Miraculous Births

¹¹ Now Abraham and Sarah were old and well stricken in age; and it ceased to be with Sarah after the manner of women.
¹² Therefore Sarah laughed within herself, saying, After I am waxed old shall I have pleasure, my lord being old also?
¹³ And the Lord said unto Abraham, Wherefore did Sarah laugh, saying, Shall I of a surety bear a child, which am old?
¹⁴ Is any thing too hard for the Lord? At the time appointed I will return unto thee, according to the time of life, and Sarah shall have a son.

### Genesis 21:1-8

²¹ And the Lord visited Sarah as he had said, and the Lord did unto Sarah as he had spoken.
² For Sarah conceived, and bare Abraham a son in his old age, at the set time of which God had spoken to him.
³ And Abraham called the name of his son that was born unto him, whom Sarah bare to him, Isaac.
⁴ And Abraham circumcised his son Isaac being eight days old, as God had commanded him.
⁵ And Abraham was an hundred years old, when his son Isaac was born unto him.
⁶ And Sarah said, God hath made me to laugh, so that all that hear will laugh with me.
⁷ And she said, Who would have said unto Abraham, that Sarah should have given children suck? for I have born him a son in his old age.
⁸ And the child grew, and was weaned: and Abraham made a great feast the same day that Isaac was weaned.

## 2. Abraham and Sarah's Bodies Restored Through Faith

### Romans 4:16-22

¹⁶ Therefore it is of faith, that it might be by grace; to the end the promise might be sure to all the seed; not to that only

which is of the law, but to that also which is of the faith of Abraham; who is the father of us all,

17 (As it is written, I have made thee a father of many nations,) before him whom he believed, even God, who quickeneth the dead, and calleth those things which be not as though they were.

18 Who against hope believed in hope, that he might become the father of many nations, according to that which was spoken, So shall thy seed be.

19 And being not weak in faith, he considered not his own body now dead, when he was about an hundred years old, neither yet the deadness of Sarah's womb:

20 He staggered not at the promise of God through unbelief; but was strong in faith, giving glory to God;

21 And being fully persuaded that, what he had promised, he was able also to perform.

22 And therefore it was imputed to him for righteousness.

## 3. Sarah Given Strength to Conceive, Abraham's Body Restored

### Hebrews 11:11-12

11 Through faith also Sara herself received strength to conceive seed, and was delivered of a child when she was past age, because she judged him faithful who had promised.

12 Therefore sprang there even of one, and him as good as dead, so many as the stars of the sky in multitude, and as the sand which is by the sea shore innumerable.

## 4. Abimelech, His Wife and Maidservants Healed (Abraham)

### Genesis 20:1-18

1 And Abraham journeyed from thence toward the south country, and dwelled between Kadesh and Shur, and sojourned in Gerar.
2 And Abraham said of Sarah his wife, She is my sister: and Abimelech king of Gerar sent, and took Sarah.
3 But God came to Abimelech in a dream by night, and said to him, Behold, thou art but a dead man, for the woman which thou hast taken; for she is a man's wife.
4 But Abimelech had not come near her: and he said, Lord, wilt thou slay also a righteous nation?
5 Said he not unto me, She is my sister? and she, even she herself said, He is my brother: in the integrity of my heart and innocency of my hands have I done this.
6 And God said unto him in a dream, Yea, I know that thou didst this in the integrity of thy heart; for I also withheld thee from sinning against me: therefore suffered I thee not to touch her.
7 Now therefore restore the man his wife; for he is a prophet, and he shall pray for thee, and thou shalt live: and if thou restore her not, know thou that thou shalt surely die, thou, and all that are thine.
8 Therefore Abimelech rose early in the morning, and called all his servants, and told all these things in their ears: and the men were sore afraid.
9 Then Abimelech called Abraham, and said unto him, What hast thou done unto us? and what have I offended thee, that thou hast brought on me and on my kingdom a great sin? thou hast done deeds unto me that ought not to be done.
10 And Abimelech said unto Abraham, What sawest thou, that thou hast done this thing?
11 And Abraham said, Because I thought, Surely the fear of God is not in this place; and they will slay me for my wife's sake.

Examples of Barren Women & Miraculous Births

12 And yet indeed she is my sister; she is the daughter of my father, but not the daughter of my mother; and she became my wife.
13 And it came to pass, when God caused me to wander from my father's house, that I said unto her, This is thy kindness which thou shalt shew unto me; at every place whither we shall come, say of me, He is my brother.
14 And Abimelech took sheep, and oxen, and menservants, and womenservants, and gave them unto Abraham, and restored him Sarah his wife.
15 And Abimelech said, Behold, my land is before thee: dwell where it pleaseth thee.
16 And unto Sarah he said, Behold, I have given thy brother a thousand pieces of silver: behold, he is to thee a covering of the eyes, unto all that are with thee, and with all other: thus she was reproved.
17 So Abraham prayed unto God: and God healed Abimelech, and his wife, and his maidservants; and they bare children.
18 For the Lord had fast closed up all the wombs of the house of Abimelech, because of Sarah Abraham's wife.

## 5. Isaac Prayed, Rebekah's Womb Restored, Jacob and Esau Born

### Genesis 25:19-28

19 And these are the generations of Isaac, Abraham's son: Abraham begat Isaac:
20 And Isaac was forty years old when he took Rebekah to wife, the daughter of Bethuel the Syrian of Padanaram, the sister to Laban the Syrian.
21 And Isaac intreated the Lord for his wife, because she was barren: and the Lord was intreated of him, and Rebekah his wife conceived.
22 And the children struggled together within her; and she said, If it be so, why am I thus? And she went to enquire of the Lord.

Examples of Barren Women & Miraculous Births

23 And the Lord said unto her, Two nations are in thy womb, and two manner of people shall be separated from thy bowels; and the one people shall be stronger than the other people; and the elder shall serve the younger.
24 And when her days to be delivered were fulfilled, behold, there were twins in her womb.
25 And the first came out red, all over like an hairy garment; and they called his name Esau.
26 And after that came his brother out, and his hand took hold on Esau's heel; and his name was called Jacob: and Isaac was threescore years old when she bare them.
27 And the boys grew: and Esau was a cunning hunter, a man of the field; and Jacob was a plain man, dwelling in tents.
28 And Isaac loved Esau, because he did eat of his venison: but Rebekah loved Jacob.

## 6. Rachel's Womb Restored, Joseph Born

### Genesis 30:1-8, 22-24

1 And when Rachel saw that she bare Jacob no children, Rachel envied her sister; and said unto Jacob, Give me children, or else I die.
2 And Jacob's anger was kindled against Rachel: and he said, Am I in God's stead, who hath withheld from thee the fruit of the womb?

22 And God remembered Rachel, and God hearkened to her, and opened her womb.
23 And she conceived, and bare a son; and said, God hath taken away my reproach:
24 And she called his name Joseph; and said, The Lord shall add to me another son.

Examples of Barren Women & Miraculous Births

# 7. Manoah's Wife's Womb Restored, Samson Born

## Judges 13:1-25

¹ And the children of Israel did evil again in the sight of the Lord; and the Lord delivered them into the hand of the Philistines forty years.
² And there was a certain man of Zorah, of the family of the Danites, whose name was Manoah; and his wife was barren, and bare not.
³ And the angel of the Lord appeared unto the woman, and said unto her, Behold now, thou art barren, and bearest not: but thou shalt conceive, and bear a son.
⁴ Now therefore beware, I pray thee, and drink not wine nor strong drink, and eat not any unclean thing:
⁵ For, lo, thou shalt conceive, and bear a son; and no razor shall come on his head: for the child shall be a Nazarite unto God from the womb: and he shall begin to deliver Israel out of the hand of the Philistines.
⁶ Then the woman came and told her husband, saying, A man of God came unto me, and his countenance was like the countenance of an angel of God, very terrible: but I asked him not whence he was, neither told he me his name:
⁷ But he said unto me, Behold, thou shalt conceive, and bear a son; and now drink no wine nor strong drink, neither eat any unclean thing: for the child shall be a Nazarite to God from the womb to the day of his death.
⁸ Then Manoah intreated the Lord, and said, O my Lord, let the man of God which thou didst send come again unto us, and teach us what we shall do unto the child that shall be born.
⁹ And God hearkened to the voice of Manoah; and the angel of God came again unto the woman as she sat in the field: but Manoah her husband was not with her.
¹⁰ And the woman made haste, and ran, and shewed her husband, and said unto him, Behold, the man hath appeared unto me, that came unto me the other day.

## Examples of Barren Women & Miraculous Births

¹¹ And Manoah arose, and went after his wife, and came to the man, and said unto him, Art thou the man that spakest unto the woman? And he said, I am.

¹² And Manoah said, Now let thy words come to pass. How shall we order the child, and how shall we do unto him?

¹³ And the angel of the Lord said unto Manoah, Of all that I said unto the woman let her beware.

¹⁴ She may not eat of any thing that cometh of the vine, neither let her drink wine or strong drink, nor eat any unclean thing: all that I commanded her let her observe.

¹⁵ And Manoah said unto the angel of the Lord, I pray thee, let us detain thee, until we shall have made ready a kid for thee.

¹⁶ And the angel of the Lord said unto Manoah, Though thou detain me, I will not eat of thy bread: and if thou wilt offer a burnt offering, thou must offer it unto the Lord. For Manoah knew not that he was an angel of the Lord.

¹⁷ And Manoah said unto the angel of the Lord, What is thy name, that when thy sayings come to pass we may do thee honour?

¹⁸ And the angel of the Lord said unto him, Why askest thou thus after my name, seeing it is secret?

¹⁹ So Manoah took a kid with a meat offering, and offered it upon a rock unto the Lord: and the angel did wonderously; and Manoah and his wife looked on.

²⁰ For it came to pass, when the flame went up toward heaven from off the altar, that the angel of the Lord ascended in the flame of the altar. And Manoah and his wife looked on it, and fell on their faces to the ground.

²¹ But the angel of the Lord did no more appear to Manoah and to his wife. Then Manoah knew that he was an angel of the Lord.

²² And Manoah said unto his wife, We shall surely die, because we have seen God.

²³ But his wife said unto him, If the Lord were pleased to kill us, he would not have received a burnt offering and a meat offering at our hands, neither would he have shewed us all

these things, nor would as at this time have told us such things as these.

24 And the woman bare a son, and called his name Samson: and the child grew, and the Lord blessed him.

25 And the Spirit of the Lord began to move him at times in the camp of Dan between Zorah and Eshtaol.

## 8. Hannah's Womb Restored, Samuel Born

### I Samuel 1:1-20, 24; 2:18-21

#### I Samuel 1:1-20, 24

1 Now there was a certain man of Ramathaimzophim, of mount Ephraim, and his name was Elkanah, the son of Jeroham, the son of Elihu, the son of Tohu, the son of Zuph, an Ephrathite:

2 And he had two wives; the name of the one was Hannah, and the name of the other Peninnah: and Peninnah had children, but Hannah had no children.

3 And this man went up out of his city yearly to worship and to sacrifice unto the Lord of hosts in Shiloh. And the two sons of Eli, Hophni and Phinehas, the priests of the Lord, were there.

4 And when the time was that Elkanah offered, he gave to Peninnah his wife, and to all her sons and her daughters, portions:

5 But unto Hannah he gave a worthy portion; for he loved Hannah: but the Lord had shut up her womb.

6 And her adversary also provoked her sore, for to make her fret, because the Lord had shut up her womb.

7 And as he did so year by year, when she went up to the house of the Lord, so she provoked her; therefore she wept, and did not eat.

8 Then said Elkanah her husband to her, Hannah, why weepest thou? and why eatest thou not? and why is thy heart grieved? am not I better to thee than ten sons?

## Examples of Barren Women & Miraculous Births

⁹ So Hannah rose up after they had eaten in Shiloh, and after they had drunk. Now Eli the priest sat upon a seat by a post of the temple of the Lord.

¹⁰ And she was in bitterness of soul, and prayed unto the Lord, and wept sore.

¹¹ And she vowed a vow, and said, O Lord of hosts, if thou wilt indeed look on the affliction of thine handmaid, and remember me, and not forget thine handmaid, but wilt give unto thine handmaid a man child, then I will give him unto the Lord all the days of his life, and there shall no razor come upon his head.

¹² And it came to pass, as she continued praying before the Lord, that Eli marked her mouth.

¹³ Now Hannah, she spake in her heart; only her lips moved, but her voice was not heard: therefore Eli thought she had been drunken.

¹⁴ And Eli said unto her, How long wilt thou be drunken? put away thy wine from thee.

¹⁵ And Hannah answered and said, No, my lord, I am a woman of a sorrowful spirit: I have drunk neither wine nor strong drink, but have poured out my soul before the Lord.

¹⁶ Count not thine handmaid for a daughter of Belial: for out of the abundance of my complaint and grief have I spoken hitherto.

¹⁷ Then Eli answered and said, Go in peace: and the God of Israel grant thee thy petition that thou hast asked of him.

¹⁸ And she said, Let thine handmaid find grace in thy sight. So the woman went her way, and did eat, and her countenance was no more sad.

¹⁹ And they rose up in the morning early, and worshipped before the Lord, and returned, and came to their house to Ramah: and Elkanah knew Hannah his wife; and the Lord remembered her.

²⁰ Wherefore it came to pass, when the time was come about after Hannah had conceived, that she bare a son, and called his name Samuel, saying, Because I have asked him of the Lord.

24 And when she had weaned him, she took him up with her, with three bullocks, and one ephah of flour, and a bottle of wine, and brought him unto the house of the Lord in Shiloh: and the child was young.

### I Samuel 2:18-21

18 But Samuel ministered before the Lord, being a child, girded with a linen ephod.
19 Moreover his mother made him a little coat, and brought it to him from year to year, when she came up with her husband to offer the yearly sacrifice.
20 And Eli blessed Elkanah and his wife, and said, The Lord give thee seed of this woman for the loan which is lent to the Lord. And they went unto their own home.
21 And the Lord visited Hannah, so that she conceived, and bare three sons and two daughters. And the child Samuel grew before the Lord.

## 9. Shunammite Woman's Womb Restored, Son Born (Elisha)

### II Kings 4:8-17

8 And it fell on a day, that Elisha passed to Shunem, where was a great woman; and she constrained him to eat bread. And so it was, that as oft as he passed by, he turned in thither to eat bread.
9 And she said unto her husband, Behold now, I perceive that this is an holy man of God, which passeth by us continually.
10 Let us make a little chamber, I pray thee, on the wall; and let us set for him there a bed, and a table, and a stool, and a candlestick: and it shall be, when he cometh to us, that he shall turn in thither.
11 And it fell on a day, that he came thither, and he turned into the chamber, and lay there.

¹² And he said to Gehazi his servant, Call this Shunammite. And when he had called her, she stood before him.
¹³ And he said unto him, Say now unto her, Behold, thou hast been careful for us with all this care; what is to be done for thee? wouldest thou be spoken for to the king, or to the captain of the host? And she answered, I dwell among mine own people.
¹⁴ And he said, What then is to be done for her? And Gehazi answered, Verily she hath no child, and her husband is old.
¹⁵ And he said, Call her. And when he had called her, she stood in the door.
¹⁶ And he said, About this season, according to the time of life, thou shalt embrace a son. And she said, Nay, my lord, thou man of God, do not lie unto thine handmaid.
¹⁷ And the woman conceived, and bare a son at that season that Elisha had said unto her, according to the time of life.

## 10. Elizabeth's Womb Restored, John the Baptist Born

### Luke 1:5-25, 41, 57-67

⁵ There was in the days of Herod, the king of Judaea, a certain priest named Zacharias, of the course of Abia: and his wife was of the daughters of Aaron, and her name was Elisabeth.
⁶ And they were both righteous before God, walking in all the commandments and ordinances of the Lord blameless.
⁷ And they had no child, because that Elisabeth was barren, and they both were now well stricken in years.
⁸ And it came to pass, that while he executed the priest's office before God in the order of his course,
⁹ According to the custom of the priest's office, his lot was to burn incense when he went into the temple of the Lord.
¹⁰ And the whole multitude of the people were praying without at the time of incense.

## Examples of Barren Women & Miraculous Births

11 And there appeared unto him an angel of the Lord standing on the right side of the altar of incense.
12 And when Zacharias saw him, he was troubled, and fear fell upon him.
13 But the angel said unto him, Fear not, Zacharias: for thy prayer is heard; and thy wife Elisabeth shall bear thee a son, and thou shalt call his name John.
14 And thou shalt have joy and gladness; and many shall rejoice at his birth.
15 For he shall be great in the sight of the Lord, and shall drink neither wine nor strong drink; and he shall be filled with the Holy Ghost, even from his mother's womb.
16 And many of the children of Israel shall he turn to the Lord their God.
17 And he shall go before him in the spirit and power of Elias, to turn the hearts of the fathers to the children, and the disobedient to the wisdom of the just; to make ready a people prepared for the Lord.
18 And Zacharias said unto the angel, Whereby shall I know this? for I am an old man, and my wife well stricken in years.
19 And the angel answering said unto him, I am Gabriel, that stand in the presence of God; and am sent to speak unto thee, and to shew thee these glad tidings.
20 And, behold, thou shalt be dumb, and not able to speak, until the day that these things shall be performed, because thou believest not my words, which shall be fulfilled in their season.
21 And the people waited for Zacharias, and marvelled that he tarried so long in the temple.
22 And when he came out, he could not speak unto them: and they perceived that he had seen a vision in the temple: for he beckoned unto them, and remained speechless.
23 And it came to pass, that, as soon as the days of his ministration were accomplished, he departed to his own house.
24 And after those days his wife Elisabeth conceived, and hid herself five months, saying,

## Examples of Barren Women & Miraculous Births

25 Thus hath the Lord dealt with me in the days wherein he looked on me, to take away my reproach among men.

41 And it came to pass, that, when Elisabeth heard the salutation of Mary, the babe leaped in her womb; and Elisabeth was filled with the Holy Ghost:

57 Now Elisabeth's full time came that she should be delivered; and she brought forth a son.

58 And her neighbours and her cousins heard how the Lord had shewed great mercy upon her; and they rejoiced with her.

59 And it came to pass, that on the eighth day they came to circumcise the child; and they called him Zacharias, after the name of his father.

60 And his mother answered and said, Not so; but he shall be called John.

61 And they said unto her, There is none of thy kindred that is called by this name.

62 And they made signs to his father, how he would have him called.

63 And he asked for a writing table, and wrote, saying, His name is John. And they marvelled all.

64 And his mouth was opened immediately, and his tongue loosed, and he spake, and praised God.

65 And fear came on all that dwelt round about them: and all these sayings were noised abroad throughout all the hill country of Judaea.

66 And all they that heard them laid them up in their hearts, saying, What manner of child shall this be! And the hand of the Lord was with him.

67 And his father Zacharias was filled with the Holy Ghost, and prophesied, saying,

Examples of Barren Women & Miraculous Births

# 11. Mary, the Mother of Jesus

Although there is no indication that Mary was ever barren, we list her story of conception here in this section as another example of where God caused a miraculous birth.

## Matthew 1:18; Luke 1:26-38

### Matthew 1:18

18 Now the birth of Jesus Christ was on this wise: When as his mother Mary was espoused to Joseph, before they came together, she was found with child of the Holy Ghost.

### Luke 1:26-38

26 And in the sixth month the angel Gabriel was sent from God unto a city of Galilee, named Nazareth,
27 To a virgin espoused to a man whose name was Joseph, of the house of David; and the virgin's name was Mary.
28 And the angel came in unto her, and said, Hail, thou that art highly favoured, the Lord is with thee: blessed art thou among women.
29 And when she saw him, she was troubled at his saying, and cast in her mind what manner of salutation this should be.
30 And the angel said unto her, Fear not, Mary: for thou hast found favour with God.
31 And, behold, thou shalt conceive in thy womb, and bring forth a son, and shalt call his name Jesus.
32 He shall be great, and shall be called the Son of the Highest: and the Lord God shall give unto him the throne of his father David:
33 And he shall reign over the house of Jacob for ever; and of his kingdom there shall be no end.
34 Then said Mary unto the angel, How shall this be, seeing I know not a man?
35 And the angel answered and said unto her, The Holy Ghost shall come upon thee, and the power of the Highest

shall overshadow thee: therefore also that holy thing which shall be born of thee shall be called the Son of God.

36 And, behold, thy cousin Elisabeth, she hath also conceived a son in her old age: and this is the sixth month with her, who was called barren.

37 For with God nothing shall be impossible.

38 And Mary said, Behold the handmaid of the Lord; be it unto me according to thy word. And the angel departed from her.

# *People Raised From the Dead*

All of the scriptures in this section are duplicated in the Old Testament and New Testament examples of healing.

## 1. Son of the Widow of Zarephath Brought Back to Life (Elijah)

### I Kings 17:17-24

17 And it came to pass after these things, that the son of the woman, the mistress of the house, fell sick; and his sickness was so sore, that there was no breath left in him.
18 And she said unto Elijah, What have I to do with thee, O thou man of God? art thou come unto me to call my sin to remembrance, and to slay my son?
19 And he said unto her, Give me thy son. And he took him out of her bosom, and carried him up into a loft, where he abode, and laid him upon his own bed.
20 And he cried unto the Lord, and said, O Lord my God, hast thou also brought evil upon the widow with whom I sojourn, by slaying her son?
21 And he stretched himself upon the child three times, and cried unto the Lord, and said, O Lord my God, I pray thee, let this child's soul come into him again.
22 And the Lord heard the voice of Elijah; and the soul of the child came into him again, and he revived.
23 And Elijah took the child, and brought him down out of the chamber into the house, and delivered him unto his mother: and Elijah said, See, thy son liveth.

24 And the woman said to Elijah, Now by this I know that thou art a man of God, and that the word of the Lord in thy mouth is truth.

## 2. Shunammite Woman's Son Raised From The Dead (Elisha)

### II Kings 4:18-37

18 And when the child was grown, it fell on a day, that he went out to his father to the reapers.
19 And he said unto his father, My head, my head. And he said to a lad, Carry him to his mother.
20 And when he had taken him, and brought him to his mother, he sat on her knees till noon, and then died.
21 And she went up, and laid him on the bed of the man of God, and shut the door upon him, and went out.
22 And she called unto her husband, and said, Send me, I pray thee, one of the young men, and one of the asses, that I may run to the man of God, and come again.
23 And he said, Wherefore wilt thou go to him to day? it is neither new moon, nor sabbath. And she said, It shall be well.
24 Then she saddled an ass, and said to her servant, Drive, and go forward; slack not thy riding for me, except I bid thee.
25 So she went and came unto the man of God to mount Carmel. And it came to pass, when the man of God saw her afar off, that he said to Gehazi his servant, Behold, yonder is that Shunammite:
26 Run now, I pray thee, to meet her, and say unto her, Is it well with thee? is it well with thy husband? is it well with the child? And she answered, It is well:
27 And when she came to the man of God to the hill, she caught him by the feet: but Gehazi came near to thrust her away. And the man of God said, Let her alone; for her soul is

## People Raised From the Dead

vexed within her: and the Lord hath hid it from me, and hath not told me.

28 Then she said, Did I desire a son of my lord? did I not say, Do not deceive me?

29 Then he said to Gehazi, Gird up thy loins, and take my staff in thine hand, and go thy way: if thou meet any man, salute him not; and if any salute thee, answer him not again: and lay my staff upon the face of the child.

30 And the mother of the child said, As the Lord liveth, and as thy soul liveth, I will not leave thee. And he arose, and followed her.

31 And Gehazi passed on before them, and laid the staff upon the face of the child; but there was neither voice, nor hearing. Wherefore he went again to meet him, and told him, saying, The child is not awaked.

32 And when Elisha was come into the house, behold, the child was dead, and laid upon his bed.

33 He went in therefore, and shut the door upon them twain, and prayed unto the Lord.

34 And he went up, and lay upon the child, and put his mouth upon his mouth, and his eyes upon his eyes, and his hands upon his hands: and stretched himself upon the child; and the flesh of the child waxed warm.

35 Then he returned, and walked in the house to and fro; and went up, and stretched himself upon him: and the child sneezed seven times, and the child opened his eyes.

36 And he called Gehazi, and said, Call this Shunammite. So he called her. And when she was come in unto him, he said, Take up thy son.

37 Then she went in, and fell at his feet, and bowed herself to the ground, and took up her son, and went out.

## 3. Dead Man Revived in Elisha's Tomb

### II Kings 13:14, 21

20 And Elisha died, and they buried him. And the bands of the Moabites invaded the land at the coming in of the year.
21 And it came to pass, as they were burying a man, that, behold, they spied a band of men; and they cast the man into the sepulchre of Elisha: and when the man was let down, and touched the bones of Elisha, he revived, and stood up on his feet.

## 4. Jesus Raises Jarius' Daughter (Synagogue Leader)

### Matthew 9:18-19, 9:23-26; Mark 5:21-24; Luke 8:40-42; 8:49-56

#### Matthew 9:18-19, 23-26

18 While he spake these things unto them, behold, there came a certain ruler, and worshipped him, saying, My daughter is even now dead: but come and lay thy hand upon her, and she shall live.
19 And Jesus arose, and followed him, and so did his disciples.

23 And when Jesus came into the ruler's house, and saw the minstrels and the people making a noise,
24 He said unto them, Give place: for the maid is not dead, but sleepeth. And they laughed him to scorn.
25 But when the people were put forth, he went in, and took her by the hand, and the maid arose.
26 And the fame hereof went abroad into all that land.

People Raised From the Dead

## Mark 5:21-24

21 And when Jesus was passed over again by ship unto the other side, much people gathered unto him: and he was nigh unto the sea.
22 And, behold, there cometh one of the rulers of the synagogue, Jairus by name; and when he saw him, he fell at his feet,
23 And besought him greatly, saying, My little daughter lieth at the point of death: I pray thee, come and lay thy hands on her, that she may be healed; and she shall live.
24 And Jesus went with him; and much people followed him, and thronged him.

Mark 5:35-43

35 While he yet spake, there came from the ruler of the synagogue's house certain which said, Thy daughter is dead: why troublest thou the Master any further?
36 As soon as Jesus heard the word that was spoken, he saith unto the ruler of the synagogue, Be not afraid, only believe.
37 And he suffered no man to follow him, save Peter, and James, and John the brother of James.
38 And he cometh to the house of the ruler of the synagogue, and seeth the tumult, and them that wept and wailed greatly.
39 And when he was come in, he saith unto them, Why make ye this ado, and weep? the damsel is not dead, but sleepeth.
40 And they laughed him to scorn. But when he had put them all out, he taketh the father and the mother of the damsel, and them that were with him, and entereth in where the damsel was lying.
41 And he took the damsel by the hand, and said unto her, Talitha cumi; which is, being interpreted, Damsel, I say unto thee, arise.
42 And straightway the damsel arose, and walked; for she was of the age of twelve years. And they were astonished with a great astonishment.

⁴³ And he charged them straitly that no man should know it; and commanded that something should be given her to eat.

## Luke 8:40-42

⁴⁰ And it came to pass, that, when Jesus was returned, the people gladly received him: for they were all waiting for him.
⁴¹ And, behold, there came a man named Jairus, and he was a ruler of the synagogue: and he fell down at Jesus' feet, and besought him that he would come into his house:
⁴² For he had one only daughter, about twelve years of age, and she lay a dying. But as he went the people thronged him.

## Luke 8:49-56

⁴⁹ While he yet spake, there cometh one from the ruler of the synagogue's house, saying to him, Thy daughter is dead; trouble not the Master.
⁵⁰ But when Jesus heard it, he answered him, saying, Fear not: believe only, and she shall be made whole.
⁵¹ And when he came into the house, he suffered no man to go in, save Peter, and James, and John, and the father and the mother of the maiden.
⁵² And all wept, and bewailed her: but he said, Weep not; she is not dead, but sleepeth.
⁵³ And they laughed him to scorn, knowing that she was dead.
⁵⁴ And he put them all out, and took her by the hand, and called, saying, Maid, arise.
⁵⁵ And her spirit came again, and she arose straightway: and he commanded to give her meat.
⁵⁶ And her parents were astonished: but he charged them that they should tell no man what was done.

## 5. People Rose From Dead When Jesus Gave Up His Spirit – and After Jesus' Resurrection

### Matthew 27:50-53

50 Jesus, when he had cried again with a loud voice, yielded up the ghost.
51 And, behold, the veil of the temple was rent in twain from the top to the bottom; and the earth did quake, and the rocks rent;
52 And the graves were opened; and many bodies of the saints which slept arose,
53 And came out of the graves after his resurrection, and went into the holy city, and appeared unto many.

## 6. Jesus Is Resurrected from the Dead

See the full account from Matthew 15:1-20; Mark 16:1-20; Luke 24:1-53; John 20:1:31 at the end of the Chapter on Examples From the New Testament – Gospels.

### Matthew 28:5-7

5 And the angel answered and said unto the women, Fear not ye: for I know that ye seek Jesus, which was crucified.
6 He is not here: for he is risen, as he said. Come, see the place where the Lord lay.
7 And go quickly, and tell his disciples that he is risen from the dead; and, behold, he goeth before you into Galilee; there shall ye see him: lo, I have told you.

## 7. Man Was Raised From The Dead

There is speculation that this man was raised from the dead.

## Mark 14:51-52

51 And there followed him a certain young man, having a linen cloth cast about his naked body; and the young men laid hold on him:
52 And he left the linen cloth, and fled from them naked.

## 8.   Jesus Raises Widow's Dead Son at Nain

### Luke 7:11-17

11 And it came to pass the day after, that he went into a city called Nain; and many of his disciples went with him, and much people.
12 Now when he came nigh to the gate of the city, behold, there was a dead man carried out, the only son of his mother, and she was a widow: and much people of the city was with her.
13 And when the Lord saw her, he had compassion on her, and said unto her, Weep not.
14 And he came and touched the bier: and they that bare him stood still. And he said, Young man, I say unto thee, Arise.
15 And he that was dead sat up, and began to speak. And he delivered him to his mother.
16 And there came a fear on all: and they glorified God, saying, That a great prophet is risen up among us; and, That God hath visited his people.
17 And this rumour of him went forth throughout all Judaea, and throughout all the region round about.

## 9.   Jesus Raises Lazarus From the Dead

### John 11:1-45

1 Now a certain man was sick, named Lazarus, of Bethany, the town of Mary and her sister Martha.

## People Raised From the Dead

2 (It was that Mary which anointed the Lord with ointment, and wiped his feet with her hair, whose brother Lazarus was sick.)

3 Therefore his sisters sent unto him, saying, Lord, behold, he whom thou lovest is sick.

4 When Jesus heard that, he said, This sickness is not unto death, but for the glory of God, that the Son of God might be glorified thereby.

5 Now Jesus loved Martha, and her sister, and Lazarus.

6 When he had heard therefore that he was sick, he abode two days still in the same place where he was.

7 Then after that saith he to his disciples, Let us go into Judaea again.

8 His disciples say unto him, Master, the Jews of late sought to stone thee; and goest thou thither again?

9 Jesus answered, Are there not twelve hours in the day? If any man walk in the day, he stumbleth not, because he seeth the light of this world.

10 But if a man walk in the night, he stumbleth, because there is no light in him.

11 These things said he: and after that he saith unto them, Our friend Lazarus sleepeth; but I go, that I may awake him out of sleep.

12 Then said his disciples, Lord, if he sleep, he shall do well.

13 Howbeit Jesus spake of his death: but they thought that he had spoken of taking of rest in sleep.

14 Then said Jesus unto them plainly, Lazarus is dead.

15 And I am glad for your sakes that I was not there, to the intent ye may believe; nevertheless let us go unto him.

16 Then said Thomas, which is called Didymus, unto his fellowdisciples, Let us also go, that we may die with him.

17 Then when Jesus came, he found that he had lain in the grave four days already.

18 Now Bethany was nigh unto Jerusalem, about fifteen furlongs off:

## People Raised From the Dead

¹⁹ And many of the Jews came to Martha and Mary, to comfort them concerning their brother.

²⁰ Then Martha, as soon as she heard that Jesus was coming, went and met him: but Mary sat still in the house.

²¹ Then said Martha unto Jesus, Lord, if thou hadst been here, my brother had not died.

²² But I know, that even now, whatsoever thou wilt ask of God, God will give it thee.

²³ Jesus saith unto her, Thy brother shall rise again.

²⁴ Martha saith unto him, I know that he shall rise again in the resurrection at the last day.

²⁵ Jesus said unto her, I am the resurrection, and the life: he that believeth in me, though he were dead, yet shall he live:

²⁶ And whosoever liveth and believeth in me shall never die. Believest thou this?

²⁷ She saith unto him, Yea, Lord: I believe that thou art the Christ, the Son of God, which should come into the world.

²⁸ And when she had so said, she went her way, and called Mary her sister secretly, saying, The Master is come, and calleth for thee.

²⁹ As soon as she heard that, she arose quickly, and came unto him.

³⁰ Now Jesus was not yet come into the town, but was in that place where Martha met him.

³¹ The Jews then which were with her in the house, and comforted her, when they saw Mary, that she rose up hastily and went out, followed her, saying, She goeth unto the grave to weep there.

³² Then when Mary was come where Jesus was, and saw him, she fell down at his feet, saying unto him, Lord, if thou hadst been here, my brother had not died.

³³ When Jesus therefore saw her weeping, and the Jews also weeping which came with her, he groaned in the spirit, and was troubled.

³⁴ And said, Where have ye laid him? They said unto him, Lord, come and see.

## People Raised From the Dead

35 Jesus wept.

36 Then said the Jews, Behold how he loved him!

37 And some of them said, Could not this man, which opened the eyes of the blind, have caused that even this man should not have died?

38 Jesus therefore again groaning in himself cometh to the grave. It was a cave, and a stone lay upon it.

39 Jesus said, Take ye away the stone. Martha, the sister of him that was dead, saith unto him, Lord, by this time he stinketh: for he hath been dead four days.

40 Jesus saith unto her, Said I not unto thee, that, if thou wouldest believe, thou shouldest see the glory of God?

41 Then they took away the stone from the place where the dead was laid. And Jesus lifted up his eyes, and said, Father, I thank thee that thou hast heard me.

42 And I knew that thou hearest me always: but because of the people which stand by I said it, that they may believe that thou hast sent me.

43 And when he thus had spoken, he cried with a loud voice, Lazarus, come forth.

44 And he that was dead came forth, bound hand and foot with graveclothes: and his face was bound about with a napkin. Jesus saith unto them, Loose him, and let him go.

45 Then many of the Jews which came to Mary, and had seen the things which Jesus did, believed on him.

## 10. Tabitha (Dorcas) Raised From Death To Life (Peter)

### Acts 9:36-42

36 Now there was at Joppa a certain disciple named Tabitha, which by interpretation is called Dorcas: this woman was full of good works and almsdeeds which she did.

## People Raised From the Dead

37 And it came to pass in those days, that she was sick, and died: whom when they had washed, they laid her in an upper chamber.

38 And forasmuch as Lydda was nigh to Joppa, and the disciples had heard that Peter was there, they sent unto him two men, desiring him that he would not delay to come to them.

39 Then Peter arose and went with them. When he was come, they brought him into the upper chamber: and all the widows stood by him weeping, and shewing the coats and garments which Dorcas made, while she was with them.

40 But Peter put them all forth, and kneeled down, and prayed; and turning him to the body said, Tabitha, arise. And she opened her eyes: and when she saw Peter, she sat up.

41 And he gave her his hand, and lifted her up, and when he had called the saints and widows, presented her alive.

42 And it was known throughout all Joppa; and many believed in the Lord.

## 11. Eutychus Raised Back to Life (Paul)

### Acts 20:6-12

6 And we sailed away from Philippi after the days of unleavened bread, and came unto them to Troas in five days; where we abode seven days.

7 And upon the first day of the week, when the disciples came together to break bread, Paul preached unto them, ready to depart on the morrow; and continued his speech until midnight.

8 And there were many lights in the upper chamber, where they were gathered together.

9 And there sat in a window a certain young man named Eutychus, being fallen into a deep sleep: and as Paul was

long preaching, he sunk down with sleep, and fell down from the third loft, and was taken up dead.
10 And Paul went down, and fell on him, and embracing him said, Trouble not yourselves; for his life is in him.
11 When he therefore was come up again, and had broken bread, and eaten, and talked a long while, even till break of day, so he departed.
12 And they brought the young man alive, and were not a little comforted.

## 12. Was Paul Healed – Or Raised from the Dead?

### Acts 20:19-20

19 And there came thither certain Jews from Antioch and Iconium, who persuaded the people, and having stoned Paul, drew him out of the city, supposing he had been dead.
20 Howbeit, as the disciples stood round about him, he rose up, and came into the city: and the next day he departed with Barnabas to Derbe.

## *About the Author (Compiler)*

The Author of *God's Healing Scriptures* is the Holy Spirit!

The scriptures were simply researched and compiled for publication in this format by Akili Kumasi.

Akili Kumasi is the founder of the God Is Love Ministries and G.I.L. Publications, a former college instructor and a Deacon in his church. He has led numerous Bible study groups, and has a deep passion to see men, husbands and fathers restored and strengthened in their marriages and families.

Kumasi is the author of several fatherhood books: *Fatherhood Principles of Joseph the Carpenter*, *On the Outside Looking In* and *Fun Meals for Fathers and Sons*. He has compiled scripture books including *God's Healing Scriptures* and the *101 In the Bible Series* (on Women, Prayers and Victories in the Bible), and has authored the internationally recognized *Bible Word Search Puzzles* series.

Kumasi earned a Bachelor's of Science from San Francisco State University in International Relations, and a Master of Science in Education from Baruch College. He also taught at Nyack College and Medgar Evers College in New York City.

Kumasi is the father of four, two sons and two daughters. He currently resides in Queens, New York with his wife, Daisy.

For more information email Kumasi@GILpublications.com.

# Do You Have a Relationship With God?

The Bible tells us that:

> *... if you confess with your mouth, "Jesus is Lord," and believe in your heart that God raised him from the dead, you will be saved.*
>
> Romans 10:9 KJV

### HAVE YOU ACCEPTED JESUS AS YOUR LORD?

If you do not have a relationship with God – through accepting Jesus as Lord – then I invite you to please pray the following prayer:

> *Lord, I come before you today to confess that I accept Jesus as my Lord and Savior and that I believe you raised Him from the dead. I believe that He died for my sins and that only through Him can I be saved.*
>
> *Lord, please forgive me of all my sins and accept me into your Kingdom. Lord, I welcome the Holy Spirit into my heart today.*
>
> *I thank you, Lord, in Jesus' Name, Amen.*

Congratulations! Now, you - as a born-again Christian can best maintain your walk with God by:

- Praying daily – ask God to help you with the challenges in your life and to bring you closer to Himself
- Read and Study God's Word (the Bible) daily
- Attend a Bible teaching church
- Fellowship with other serious Christians

A good place to start your Bible reading is with the book of John.

If you have questions or need help please write to me at:

Akili Kumasi
**GOD IS LOVE MINISTRIES**
P.O. Box 80275, Brooklyn, NY 11208
kumasi@GILpublications.com

# G.I.L. PUBLICATIONS.com
## Quick Order Form – *Page 1*

Mail Order .........................GIL Publications
P. O. Box 80275, Brooklyn, NY 11208
Telephone Orders.................(718) 386-6434
Website Orders ....................www.GILpublications.com

| SCRIPTURE REFERENCE BOOKS |||||
|---|---|---|---|
| **Book Title** | Price | # | Total |
| **God's Healing Scriptures** 240 Prayers & Promises in the Bible | $9.95 | | |
| 101 Women in the Bible | $6.95 | | |
| 101 Prayers in the Bible | $6.95 | | |
| 101 Victories in the Bible | $6.95 | | |
| **HALL OF FAITH CLASSICS** ||||
| *Volume 1: The Person and Work of the Holy Spirit* (R.A. Torrey) | $9.75 | | |
| *Volume 2: How to Pray* (R.A. Torrey) | $5.95 | | |
| *Volume 3: How To Obtain the Fullness of Power for Life and Christian Service* (R.A. Torrey) | $5.75 | | |
| *Volume 4: Absolute Surrender* (Andrew Murray) | $6.25 | | |
| *Volume 5: Humility: The Beauty of Holiness* (Andrew Murray) | $5.75 | | |
| Hall of Faith 5-Pack (Volumes 1, 2, 3, 4, 5) – $25% off – Save $8.35 | $25.10 | | |
| **FATHERHOOD BOOKS** ||||
| Fatherhood Principles of Joseph the Carpenter | $8.95 | | |
| Fun Meals for Fathers and Sons | $4.95 | | |
| On the Outside Looking In | $7.95 | | |

To pay by Credit / Debit Card – go to www.GILpublications.com or call 718-386-6434

# Complete the Order Form on the next page

# G.I.L. PUBLICATIONS.com
## Quick Order Form – *Page 2*

Mail Order .......................... GIL Publications
                                     P. O. Box 80275, Brooklyn, NY 11208
Telephone Orders ............... (718) 386-6434
Website Orders ................... www.GILpublications.com

| Book Title | Price | # | Total |
|---|---|---|---|
| **Bible Word Search** – Puzzles with Scriptures (80 puzzles per book) ||||
| Vol. I: **Extracts** from the Bible | $7.95 | | |
| Vol. II: **Women** in the Bible | $7.95 | | |
| Vol. III: **Fathers** in the Bible | $7.95 | | |
| Vol. IV: **Prayers** in the Bible | $7.95 | | |
| Vol. V: **Victories** in the Bible | $7.95 | | |
| Vol. VI: **Parables** in the Bible | $7.95 | | |
| Vol. VII: **Promises** in the Bible | $7.95 | | |
| Vol. VIII: **Foundations** in Christianity **(100 Puzzles)** | $8.95 | | |
| **Bible Word Search 8-Pack (all 8 books)** *– 17% off – Save $11.00* | $53.62 | | |
| Bible Word Search, **Large Print, No. 1** | $5.95 | | |
| **Church Edition CD  - *560 puzzles –*** (7 volumes, lesson plans, group activities) | $5.95 | | |
| EDUCATOR'S WORD SEARCH Vol. 1: U.S. Presidents | $5.95 | | |
| Sub-Total ||| |
| NY Residents Add 8.5% Tax ||| |
| Shipping ($3.95 1st item, 50¢ each additional) ||| |
| *TOTAL* ||| |

Date:_____   Payment: ▣ Check  ▣ Money Order
Name:_____
Address:_____
City:_____ State:_____ Zip:_____
Telephone:_____
E-Mail:_____

Printed in Great Britain
by Amazon